Billy Graham
Evangelistic Association

1 Billy Gra

D0462180

DEAR FRIEND:

I am pleased to send you this copy of *Boxers to Bandits*.

My mother, Ruth Bell Graham, was born in China. Her father was a missionary doctor who went to China in the early 1900s, a few years after that country's infamous Boxer Rebellion. My grandparents lived and worked in the same city as Jimmy and Sophie Graham (no relation), an American couple who had arrived a quarter century earlier. My mother grew up calling them "Uncle Jimmy" and "Aunt Sophie" and was greatly influenced by their love for Jesus and their life of joyful sacrifice and service.

This is a remarkable story of adventure and perseverance, a story of lives lived well for God. I trust that you will be inspired and strengthened in your faith.

If you would like to know more about the Billy Graham Evangelistic Association, please contact us. We would appreciate knowing how this book or our ministry has touched your life.

May God bless you.

Sincerely,

Franklin Graham
President

"This is an astonishing account of some extraordinary servants of the Gospel. It deserves a place in the annals of great missionary endeavors."

—Dr. Duane Litfin, president,
Wheaton College, Wheaton, Ill.

"My wife and I were deeply moved as we read the story of Jimmy and Sophie Graham. We both recommend this volume to the church that again needs to be encouraged both in the grace of our Lord Jesus and the fellowship of the Gospel ... "

—Dr. Walter C. Kaiser, Jr., president,
Gordon-Conwell Seminary, South Hamilton, Mass.

"These two lived life as it should be lived, flat out for Christ! Their stirring biographical report got to me. I want this for you too."

—Raymond C. Ortlund, author
and director, Renewal Ministries, Newport Beach, Calif.

" ... Reverend and Mrs. Graham were truly missionaries in the highest sense. The Grahams ministered to many Chinese in loving care and instruction, not asking for recognition or acclaim. The book gives a history of not only this grand missionary family but also the movement of the Gospel through the villages, towns, and universities of China in the late nineteenth and early twentieth centuries ... "

—Dr. Sophie Wong, city councilwoman,
daughter of book characters Calvin and Sophie Chao

"I have yet to see a biography more absorbing, more graphic, more intense. Here is a deeply meaningful account wrapped in brilliant writing!"

—Ralph Winter, former director,
U.S. Center for World Mission, Pasadena, Calif.

"Each succeeding generation needs to hear the story of Jimmy and Sophie Graham. Their 'living sacrifice,' though costly, and at times seemingly futile, has resulted in an amazing harvest of souls in northern China. I know. I have been there and seen the results."

—Dr. George W. Murray, president,
Columbia International University, Columbia, S.C.

"Who could have known one hundred years ago the spiritual harvest of these lives, sown in Chinese soil to die and be raised to life, as millions of Chinese today follow the ways of Yesu?"

—Charlie Davis, executive director,
TEAM Mission

"The story of the Grahams has certainly encouraged me as well as humbled me and strengthened my resolve to faithful and joyful service in spite of the obstacles."

—Robert Cannada, Jr., chancellor
and CEO, Reformed Theological Seminary, Charlotte, N.C.

"This story illustrates not only the enormous challenges confronting missionaries during this turbulent time, but, far more significantly, their indefatigable commitment to the Lord Jesus Christ."

—Dr. Harold Netland, professor of philosophy of religion and
intercultural studies, Trinity Evangelical Divinity School, Deerfield, Ill.

"My prayer is that God will use this book, not only to encourage us concerning the past, but also to raise up a whole generation of those who are willing to sacrifice themselves that others might experience the freedom that comes through the gospel of our Lord Jesus Christ."

—Paul Kooistra, coordinator,
Mission to the World, Lawrenceville, Ga.

"In an age when emotion seems to outweigh commitment, it is an encouragement to read of the real heroes of the faith and their sacrifice. I would like for every teen missionary to read this book."

—Robert M. Bland, executive director,
Teen Missions International

"Jimmy and Sophie Graham will astonish you, challenge, inspire. They have me! Steve Fortosis has researched those pioneer days like a true historian and tells this heroic story with a magic that draws you into it. A powerful story, well told."

—Robertson McQuilkin, president emeritus,
Columbia International University, Columbia, S.C.

"I have known three generations of the Graham family, and to have this story is a great gift to present-day Christendom. I am so happy to know the book is now in the making."

—Sanna B. Rossi, author

"The Graham family, which spans five generations of remarkable Christian workers reaching back into the nineteenth century, must be one of the best kept secrets of modern missions. The ministries of the three James Grahams plus their families have impacted profoundly the church of Jesus Christ."

—David M. Howard, former international director,
World Evangelical Fellowship, and president, Latin America Mission

BOXERS TO BANDITS

THE EXTRAORDINARY STORY OF

JIMMY AND SOPHIE GRAHAM,

PIONEER MISSIONARIES IN CHINA,

1889–1940

BY
STEPHEN FORTOSIS

BASED ON ARCHIVES COMPILED BY
MARY GRAHAM REID

THIS BILLY GRAHAM LIBRARY SELECTION SPECIAL EDITION IS
PUBLISHED BY THE BILLY GRAHAM EVANGELISTIC ASSOCIATION

A *Billy Graham Library Selection* designates materials that are appropriate to a well-rounded collection of quality Christian literature, including both classic and contemporary reading and reference materials.

Published by the Billy Graham Evangelistic Association, Charlotte, North Carolina.

Scripture quotations marked KJV are taken from the King James Version.

Scripture quotations marked NKJV are taken from the New King James Version. ©1982 by Thomas Nelson, Inc. Used by permission. All rights reserved.

Scripture quotations marked NLT are taken from the *Holy Bible,* New Living Translation, ©1996. Used by permission of Tyndale House Publishers, Inc., Wheaton, Illinois 60189. All rights reserved.

Photos are from the collections of Mary Graham Reid, Virginia Bell Somerville, and Sandy Yates Gartrell.

Cover and interior design by John Jung
Map illustrations by John Jung and Jarod Sutphin

ISBN 1-59328-068-8

DEDICATION

To all Christian
missionaries, pastors, and believers
who have suffered persecution
or have lost their lives in China
as a result of their commitment
to Christ.

"They climbed
the steep ascent to heaven
through peril, toil, and pain.
O God,
to us,
may grace be given
to follow in their train."[1]

CONTENTS

Foreword by Ruth Bell Graham.................................xiii

Acknowledgments..xv

Introduction...xvii

Maps...2

Chapter 1   Roots..9

Chapter 2   Boxers...23

Chapter 3   Harvest..45

Chapter 4   Prayer...57

Chapter 5   Fruit..71

Chapter 6   Bandits..87

Chapter 7   Famine...101

Chapter 8   Martyrs..117

Chapter 9   Baptized!..137

Chapter 10 Legacy...159

Afterword by J. Robertson McQuilkin...........................187

Endnotes & Bibliography..199

China Stories by James R. Graham III...........................209

The Old Manse (appendix).......................................287

FOREWORD

Though Uncle Jimmy and Aunt Sophie Graham were not kin, they were closer to me, by far, than my own grandparents. This was because, throughout my childhood and teen years, my family lived as their neighbors and coworkers on the same mission station in China. We were with them seven years at a stretch, followed by a one-year furlough.

Uncle Jimmy opened our station in China together with Pearl Buck's father, Absalom Sydenstricker. I remember Aunt Sophie telling me once that when Uncle Jimmy returned from the countryside, where he had been preaching the Gospel, there was not one place on his body where she could lay her hands that was not black and blue with bruises where he had been stoned.

He went for years without one conversion. I remember asking him if he ever got discouraged. He shook his head, emphatically replying, "No, the battle is the Lord's and He will deliver the victory into our hands."

The last time I visited China, I had the opportunity of sitting in their old home, which had been made into a wholesale grocery outlet during the Cultural Revolution. At that time I was told there were around 300,000 believers in that same countryside where Uncle Jimmy had ministered long before.

It is my prayer that this book will encourage and challenge both missionaries and believers from every walk of life.

—RUTH BELL GRAHAM

ACKNOWLEDGMENTS

First, ultimate thanks must go to God, who was, without doubt, working powerfully behind the scenes throughout the research, writing, and publishing of this book.

Mary Graham Reid spent considerable time researching her grandparents' lives and ministry and with the help of her husband, John, was of indispensable assistance. Others in the Graham family also contributed helpful information. Dr. and Mrs. David Baker of Conway, Arkansas, deserve credit for providing momentum by organizing and typing the Graham letters.

I'd like to express gratefulness to all those at BGEA who were involved in the initial approvals, the design, and the editing of the project. No author could ask for a more professional, supportive, or flexible staff than those serving there.

We are thankful to Christian leaders who read the first chapters of this project and urged that we move forward. Appreciation also goes to Virginia Bell Somerville and Sandy Yates Gartrell for anecdotes, details, and photos of mission work in China. We are most grateful to Ruth Bell Graham, who first suggested that this story be written, wrote the foreword, and recommended the book's title.

—STEPHEN FORTOSIS

INTRODUCTION

By John Reid

"O Zion, haste,
thy mission high fulfilling,
to tell to all the world
that God is Light."[1]

This book is primarily about my wife's grandparents and, because it is the story of a family, also about her father. My first introduction to Mary, who compiled the archives upon which this book is based, was through hearing her gifted father, Dr. James Graham III, preach while on an extended furlough during his 60 years of missionary endeavor in China and Taiwan. I was attending a Christian college to prepare for a lifetime commitment to missions. Subsequent to hearing Dr. Graham speak, I met Mary and found out she was not interested in any dating relationship that didn't include going to the mission field. That was fine with me!

I then had the opportunity of meeting Mary's grandfather, Jimmy Graham II, who had just returned from China. I still remember how surprised I was when, after he left the area, I started receiving letters from him. After his death, I became aware that he wrote to many young people, and during the preparation for this book, Mary and I enjoyed reading his answers to many letters.

After my service in the U.S. Navy during World War II, Mary and I were married and entered a famous old seminary located in the South. The church history professor became my favorite teacher.

When this well-versed connoisseur of church leaders realized that Mary was a direct descendant of Thomas E. Peck, he raved to other professors that they had on their campus the great-granddaughter of Dr. Peck, one of the seven "divines" (founders) of the old Southern Presbyterian Church.

In our preparation to become missionaries, the greatest help we received came from Mary's father. His dynamic personality, his love for God's Word, and his total commitment to the cause of foreign missions had an influence on us beyond any other. While "watching and waiting," he gave himself fully to warning of the wrath to come for all those outside Christ. He was the embodiment of the true "wartime mentality" when it came to missions.

As this book progressed, it became clear to Mary that the story of her grandparents should have an afterword telling about their son. The person most suited to write about James III was Robertson McQuilkin, president emeritus of Columbia International University. When asked if he would be willing to do this, he replied that he'd "consider it an honor to write about my beloved Dr. Jim." You will enjoy his part in this book as you see how the generations followed their parents and grandparents in serving the Lord.

Miss Sophie Graham, my wife's aunt and the third daughter of Jimmy and Sophie, also served faithfully in China for a number of years, as well as in the Philippines. After having to return to America, she taught Bible classes in various places in the South. To this day many remember her dynamic Bible teaching and strong emphasis on foreign missions. Though she lived to age 103 and became a bit senile, she could always recall Scripture and hymns that had been a part of her life. She had a deep and abiding love for her parents and loved to talk about their influence in her life. Her love for her Lord was obvious to all who knew her. She truly "followed in His train."

Missionaries were not allowed into China after 1949, so Mary and I departed in 1952 for Japan to begin our 36 years of service in that great country. On our furloughs we would visit some of Mary's family members, and this added many layers of my appreciation for her grandparents, known fondly to other missionaries as "Uncle Jimmy" and "Aunt Sophie."

Mary began collecting extensive original resources surrounding their remarkable missionary career. I was a history major in college, and as I started putting this story together in my mind, it became clear that if there was ever a unique story about missions, it would be the story you are about to read.

It is a story that has deep Southern roots, dating back to a prominent colonial Williamsburg family. As a person interested in the Civil War, I was also captivated by the fact that her grandparents grew up during the Reconstruction following that war. In fact, her grandfather was reared in a Winchester, Virginia, manse that Stonewall Jackson called "home" during his Valley of Virginia campaigns.

The more I learned, the more I realized how unusual their call to China was in their day. They went to China in 1889, well before the devastating Boxer Rebellion of 1900. They lived there during World War I, the Sino-Japanese War, and the beginning days of World War II. In spite of the many difficult experiences and what for many people would have been overwhelming discouragement, they pressed on, faithful to their calling.

The China of today is a far cry from the China of Jimmy and Sophie's era. Imagine their astonishment if they could return to China in the 21st century. They would hear and see preparations for the 2008 Olympic Games in Beijing, where whole sections of the old city are being rebuilt. In old Shanghai, they would see huge new buildings, one of which is in a race to become the tallest building in the world. They would read in the newspapers about China's space exploration and her part in the nuclear arms race.

If they visited the Grand Canal, upon which they traveled many times, people all around them today would be talking about the positive and negative aspects of the largest dam in the world, being built north of where they had lived on the Yangtze River. Word would surely have reached them that Mao Tse-Tung, former head of the Chinese Communist Party, had changed the church building Uncle Jimmy helped build into a dance hall for his private entertainment.

Yes, changes everywhere, but the change which would bring overflowing joy would be the fulfillment of the Great Commission through the Chinese churches' current "Back to Jerusalem" movement. The Grahams' daughter Sophie was involved in those early prayer meetings in the 1930s where the vision of Acts 1:8 in reverse first came to Chinese believers and missionaries meeting in Shanghai to pray and plan—and then later through a very special work of the Holy Spirit at the Chinese Northwest Bible Institute.

Today, books and documentaries such as *The Cross, The Soul of China, Chinese Intellectuals and the Gospel,* and *Jesus in Beijing* reveal the astounding spread of Christianity throughout China.

In fact, in his book *Jesus in Beijing,* journalist David Aikman writes, "It is worth considering the possibility that not just the numerical, but the intellectual center of gravity for Christianity may move decisively out of Europe and North America as the Christianization of China continues and as China becomes a global superpower."[2]

In her foreword to this book, Ruth Bell Graham tells of asking Uncle Jimmy if he was ever discouraged. His response represented his heart: "The battle is the Lord's and He will deliver the victory into our hands." During my two terms in Japan as field chairman, on occasion I would mention to a fellow missionary this lesson from Mary's grandfather in China, that the battle is the Lord's. I especially recall one young man who gave up much to become a missionary to Japan. He was experiencing some of the stress so common in the life of a missionary. Mary repeated her grandfather's favorite words of encouragement. Since that time he has thanked her more than once for the help that was to him, especially as his wife suffered the ravages of cancer.

As Mary and I approached retirement, we reflected positively on the various types of service we'd engaged in during our years in Japan—opportunities in teaching, literature, and field administration. However, just as with Mary's grandfather in China, our basic call had been to church planting. This we did in the city of Yokosuka, south of Yokohama. When we first went there after a term in Tokyo, there was only one evangelical church, meeting in an antiquated building on leased land.

Yokosuka today is a very modern city of over one-half million people, now with seven evangelical churches. We did not establish all seven of the churches; other missionaries and gifted pastors were involved. Over 600 adults and young people now meet regularly in these churches, for which we praise the Lord. All of the churches have their own well-trained pastors. Our prayer as we retired was that the Lord, in the next 60 years, would be pleased to do also in Japan what Ruth Bell Graham reports has occurred in the past 60 years in the region of China where Mary's grandparents labored—the growth of the church from a small band to over 300,000 believers.

When Mary and our daughter visited that same part of China in 1987, they heard from local believers a significantly higher figure than 300,000. The exact numbers are not important, but the growth must be a great joy to the Lord of the Harvest. If this book encourages you to join us in prayer, it will be worth many times more than the considerable effort required to bring it to you.

As mentioned, this book is in many ways unusual. It is the story of a family, going back to Dr. Thomas Peck, the seminary professor, and to the Reverend James Graham I, a greatly admired Presbyterian minister. You will read that from 1889 the son and daughter of the Pecks and Grahams served in China for what would total a combined 100 years. Their direct descendants and spouses have spent another 300 years as missionaries in Asia. This comes to a total of about 400 years given to fulfill the Great Commission. It is also significant to note that there are now five family graves in Asia—in mainland China, on the island of Formosa, and in Japan, including that of our daughter, who died suddenly at age 16.

Our first daughter, born in Japan, now serves there with her family as a fourth generation missionary. Our son and his family served in the Philippines until a health problem made it necessary for them to return to America. Other descendants of the James Grahams have been involved in short-term mission trips.

Mary and I can say from the depths of our hearts that we are, beyond what words can express, grateful for the opportunity God gave us to serve Him in Asia as church planters. And if through reading this book God speaks to you about a deeper involvement in foreign missions—count it all joy. Whatever the "call" may be, please enter into the deeper meaning of lives given over to the service of the King, as reflected in this book about Uncle Jimmy and Aunt Sophie, who were humble, unselfish servant leaders.

Finally, both Mary and I want to say how much we appreciate the co-authorship of Dr. Steve Fortosis in the writing of this book. Without his writing skills, spiritual insight, and identification with the mission of this book begun over twenty years ago, it would not be in your hands. To God be the glory.

"Give of thy sons to bear
the message glorious;
Give of thy wealth to speed them
on their way;
Pour out thy soul for them
in prayer victorious;
And all thou spendest
Jesus will repay."[3]

JAMES R. GRAHAM II IN CHINA.

WHERE THE STORY TAKES PLACE

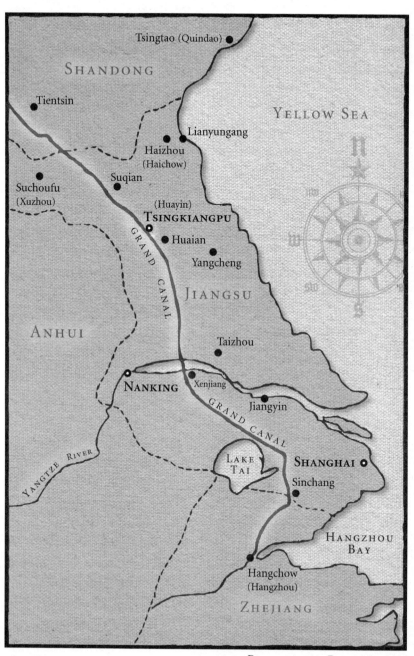

SHANDONG

Tsingtao (Quindao)

YELLOW SEA

Tientsin

Lianyungang

Haizhou
(Haichow)

Suqian

Suchoufu
(Xuzhou)

(Huayin)

TSINGKIANGPU

Huaian

Yangcheng

JIANGSU

ANHUI

GRAND CANAL

Taizhou

NANKING

Xenjiang

GRAND CANAL

Jiangyin

Yangtze River

LAKE
TAI

SHANGHAI

Sinchang

HANGZHOU
BAY

Hangchow
(Hangzhou)

ZHEJIANG

------- PROVINCIAL BOUNDARIES
━━━━━ GRAND CANAL

3

"MIDDLECOURT," THE HOUSE ON THE CAMPUS OF HAMPDEN-SYDNEY COLLEGE
IN WHICH SOPHIE WAS BORN AND WHICH REMAINED HER HOME UNTIL SHE
MARRIED AND DEPARTED FOR CHINA.

E. Berkeley.

STAUNTON, VA

Sophie Peck and Jimmy Graham exchanged photos as their romance blossomed. On the back of this 1880s photo Sophie wrote, "Taken in Staunton soon after we first met."

On the back of Jimmy's photo are the words, in his handwriting, "Most affectionately, James R Graham Jr."

SOPHIE AND JIMMY GRAHAM'S FIRST CHILD, GEORGIA (AFFECTIONATELY KNOWN AS GEORGIE), WAS BORN IN CHINA.

LORD,

I GIVE UP ALL MY OWN PLANS AND PURPOSES,

ALL MY OWN DESIRES AND HOPES

AND ACCEPT THY WILL FOR MY LIFE.

I GIVE MYSELF, MY LIFE, MY ALL

UTTERLY TO THEE TO BE THINE FOREVER.

FILL ME AND SEAL ME WITH THY HOLY SPIRIT,

USE ME AS THOU WILT, SEND ME WHERE THOU WILT,

WORK OUT THY WHOLE WILL IN MY LIFE

AT ANY COST NOW AND FOREVER.

—JIMMY GRAHAM

CHAPTER 1

ROOTS

The missionary couple had been in China for several years without a single convert. At times ugly rumors about them started in one corner of a town and quickly spiraled out of control. If a Chinese parent lost an infant, it was often assumed that these "outside barbarians" had kidnapped the child from those of the "inside kingdom," as villagers liked to call themselves.

One day word spread through town that a young Chinese child was missing. The chief of police came to Jimmy and Sophie Graham's home, and the missionaries graciously served him tea. The chief haltingly explained that the viceroy of Nanking had ordered that he search their home for a kidnapped child. Jimmy graciously escorted the man through all the rooms, opening drawers and trunks, even insisting he look under the beds. After an hour or so, the official said with evident surprise, "Why, there isn't a Chinese baby on the entire premises."

But as the official left the home, some citizens saw him and quickly assumed he'd found a dead child. Graham smiled at the group that was forming at his gate and called out words of friendship in clumsy Chinese, but more townsfolk gathered, and their mumblings rapidly turned ugly.

Several ringleaders worked up the mob to fever pitch. Bursting through the flimsy gate, they stormed the yard, moving to encircle the man, who quickly stepped to the side and stood with his back against a wall. A dead puppy sailed through the air, smacking him in the head and slinging drops of blood in his face. Men and boys with bamboo poles jabbed at his head and body or swung the poles and whacked him. A stone was hurled, striking him just below the ear. One bold woman darted close and landed a glob of saliva on his face.

His wife was secluded upstairs. Her eyes flitted to Georgie, her infant daughter. She flinched and clutched at the baby. Then with a prayer of desperation, she turned the child and held her up to the window. The little girl laughed, clapped her little hands, and waved. Down below, her father ducked as a rock smacked the house just above his head. …

When Jimmy Graham II was born on October 19, 1863, just a few months after the Battle of Gettysburg, his parents surely had no inkling that he would spend 50 years of his life as a missionary in a spot on the globe about as far away as one can be from the old homestead in northern Virginia.

You see, Jimmy's family roots were of proud Virginia blood, and Virginians of such loyalty usually stayed put. His parents were James R. Graham I and Fanny Tucker Graham. The Tuckers were prominent leaders all the way back to colonial Williamsburg. St. George Tucker saw action as a lieutenant colonel in the Revolutionary War, was a professor of law at the College of William and Mary in Williamsburg, and was named to the Virginia Court of Appeals and the Federal Bench.[1]

His son, Nathaniel Tucker, was friend and advisor to American presidents, fought in the War of 1812, played an important part in the formation and development of the State of Missouri, and trained a whole generation of leaders of the South at the College of William and Mary.[2]

In the cemetery next to the old church in Colonial Williamsburg, there is a large obelisk which marks the final resting place of a prominent member of the Tucker family. Next to the obelisk is a memorial stone upon which are engraved the words, "The Best Blood in Virginia." It is no wonder that when Jimmy II and his wife eventually went to China, it was joked that they left one place where people worshipped their ancestors only to sail to another.

Jimmy's own father, James Robert Graham I, settled in the lush Shenandoah Valley of Virginia before the American Civil War. In 1851 he began as pastor of the Kent Street Church in Winchester. Late in the same year Miss Fanny Bland Tucker Magill, great-granddaughter of the chief justice of Virginia, joined the Kent Street Church by letter from the First Church, Richmond. *A History of the Presbyterian Church in Winchester* notes dryly, "the minister courted her under the eyes and with the evident approbation of his congregation and when he married her on October 3, 1853, it gave him an extra $150.00 on that year's stipend."[3]

Upon the announcement of the upcoming marriage, the Kent Street Church decided to provide the couple with a parsonage because, according to church minutes, congregations had begun to realize that "their duties to their ministers, if they wished to keep them free from worldly cares, included a comfortable dwelling among them, rent-free and that good living conditions were essential to secure performance in pastoral relations."[4]

For the following 48 years of his lengthy pastorate and until his death in 1914, the large manse on North Braddock Street was the home of the Reverend and Mrs. James Graham I.

It wasn't a coincidence that two Graham sons became pastors, a third (James II) became a missionary to China, and the other two served as faithful church leaders. The Graham home in which Jimmy II grew up was a place in which the children daily saw Christ in their parents' hospitality, kindness to the poor, and loving discipline toward the children.

Tucker, one of Jimmy's brothers, wrote in the early 1900s and in slightly Victorian prose, "There was gladness as well as goodness there. Wit and wisdom were finely blended, and a sense of the responsibilities of life was mingled with the radiant joy of living. The genial humor of the father, the rippling laughter of the mother, together with the banter of the younger household members, lent brightness and color to the life of a home in which duty was the watchword, integrity the rule of conduct, and faith in God the motivating power."[5]

The pastorate of Dr. James Graham I was characterized by remarkable piety. Preparatory to communion each month, the minister encouraged fasting and prayer. He labored long over his sermons because of the conviction that a message that had not wearied the preacher in its preparation was sure to weary the people in its delivery. His sermons were forceful and scholarly as well as highly practical and helpful.

Graham was also careful to observe a mid-week prayer service at which it was his custom to offer an explanatory lecture, usually in the form of systematic exposition of the Bible rather than a topical sermon. Quite often, before or after the mid-week service he met with Sunday school teachers to review the lesson for the following Sabbath and coach them by means of a general discussion.

Mrs. Graham did not simply voice a theory of Christlikeness; she clothed it in flesh and blood. She awoke in those around her a longing to make her faith their own. Totally devoted to her children, only the fact that she was able to do a number of tasks at once made it possible for her to accomplish obligations at home as well as assist her husband in ministry. A friend once reported after visiting their home that she found Fanny Graham with her lap full of sewing and her foot rocking a dozing baby while she was being read to by an older child and another child recited at intervals her hymns and catechism.

Fanny shared in much of the work of her husband's ministry. She even accompanied him on pastoral rounds and in his absence went alone to visit the sick and sorrowing. One of her children later wrote, "Wherever the shadows of grief or trial fell thickest, there she came with the radiance of her gracious spirit to cheer and to help."

The secret of her character was her early morning prayer times. At a rocking chair in the corner of her bedroom she knelt and poured out her soul. Her son Jimmy rushed into his mother's room one morning to find her upon her knees. Awed, he tried to withdraw without disturbing her. But as he closed the door he heard his own name and was thrilled to realize she was in the midst of praying for him. He never forgot that moment.

By the beginning of the Civil War in 1861 the Grahams were busy rearing three of their eventual five sons and two daughters. Late that year, Confederate General Stonewall Jackson moved his base of operations to Winchester and, at some point, attended worship services at Kent Street Presbyterian and met Pastor Graham.

When Jackson declared to his forces a particular day as an occasion for humiliation and prayer, Graham scheduled a church service that day with a certain amount of trepidation. Anti-Northern feelings were running extremely high, and with many recuperating Confederate soldiers in Winchester, Graham feared the service might explode into a blasphemous tirade against the Union. He thought he'd selected an even-tempered church member to offer the opening prayer, but soon the man "was telling the Lord with singular distinctness what sort of people were making war upon us, and how He ought to let our armies deal with them." A low, rising rumble of angry voices could be heard among the congregation. Then Jackson entered the rear of the sanctuary. In desperation, following a hymn, Graham asked him to lead in prayer. Caught by surprise, the general finally stood and, confessing the unworthiness of everyone as sinners and their absolute dependence upon God's mercy, begged divine help for the afflicted nation.

Graham was impressed. Not a single word did Jackson speak which was inconsistent with the command to love one's enemies, and not once did he seek to tell God what He must do in this great crisis. The remainder of the service passed in an air of newfound reverence.[6]

On New Year's Day of 1862, Jackson rode to the Graham manse and said to the couple, "I shall have to be absent for an uncertain period. Mrs. Jackson is a stranger and will be very lonely at the hotel; will you not take her into your home? You know she is a minister's daughter and will be very happy with you."[7]

Of course, the Grahams were more than willing to comply.

Upon his return some weeks later, Jackson appeared again at the home and approached Fanny Graham with another request. "Mrs. Graham, my wife has been so happy here; will you not let her stay with you—and lest she give you any trouble, I'll just come along and help you take care of her."

General Jackson then moved from his quarters nearby into the Grahams' home for some weeks between war campaigns.

James and Fanny Graham were perfect hosts, and the Jacksons rewarded their hospitality with gratefulness and warm courtesy. Pastor Graham quickly came to consider Stonewall Jackson a member of the family. He stated, "[Jackson] ate every day at my table, slept every night under my roof, and bowed with us morning and evening at our family altar. He called my house his home."

At times Jackson discussed war matters privately with Graham, but the family usually saw a far different side of the man than did soldiers and other commanders on the battlefield. He loved children and would fuss over the Graham young ones, hugging them and trying to amuse them. When he made a child laugh, it seemed to give him special pleasure. Often at mealtimes he would enter the dining room on his hands and knees, neighing loudly like a horse while little Alfred Graham sat on his back squealing with delight.

Historian James Robertson writes of one evening when a group of young artillery officers called to pay their respects to Mrs. Jackson. Fun-loving by nature, the Confederates were soon using the chairs as cannons and waging an artillery battle with the Graham children. The antics in the parlor were robust and loud. Soon the door opened, and a stern Jackson stepped into the room. Everyone froze in embarrassment. Catching the gist of what was taking place, with mock authority the general said, "Captain Marye, report this engagement tomorrow—along with the casualties." He then took a seat to enjoy the revelry.[8]

Certainly the Graham home and family provided an ideal setting for Jackson and his wife to enjoy fully this rare experience of togetherness in the midst of chaos and wartime violence. The Christian warmth, happiness, and Southern hospitality were ingredients that brought out the tender side of Stonewall Jackson.[9]

Later, when Anna Jackson left the Grahams and returned to her home, Fanny kept up a steady correspondence with her. Fanny wrote of her life with Pastor Graham, her youngsters, Annie and Alfred, and of Jimmy II, who was still a baby and was "beginning to laugh and crow, which makes him interesting."[10]

When General Jackson was struck down by friendly fire in 1863, Anna Jackson confided in a letter to Fanny, "There was no distinction in this world I thought too high for him [her husband], for I never knew his equal in nobleness and elevation of character— but much as I admired these qualities, I trust I prized still more his whole-souled devotion to the Savior, his deep fervent piety. It was this that bound me to him with the strongest cords and made him my spiritual guide, my comforter in all trials."[11]

Fanny replied in a June 1863 letter: "Every heart bleeds at his loss. … He was more remarkable than anyone I have ever known. He seemed to be jealous for God, never allowing anyone to speak of his work, disclaiming all merit and attributing all to the work of

God—this is what made him so precious to us all and makes his loss so irreparable. But, my precious friend, it is for you that my heart bleeds—such a grief as this you could never bear but for the grace of God strengthening you." [12]

This is the home in which Jimmy Graham II grew up. He later declared that it was the spiritual nurture and love of his parents that helped motivate him to commit his life to Christ.

A powerful motivating experience occurred at age 14 when Jimmy read the biography of Henry Martyn, missionary in the early 1800s to India and Persia. The story of Martyn's life had a lasting impact on young Jimmy, shaping his heart in ways that would only become apparent over time.

Born in Cornwall, England, in 1781, Martyn had turned from agnosticism as a college student and become a Christian. His own hero was David Brainerd, a self-sacrificing American missionary to Indians during the colonial era, a man known for his extraordinary commitment to prayer. In the biography, Jimmy Graham read how Martyn, inspired by Brainerd's example, began spending many hours daily in prayer and devotions. He dedicated his life to missions and sailed in 1810 for Persia (Iran) where he performed the remarkable task of translating the New Testament into Hindustani, Persian, and Arabic. [13]

But it was the great heart of Henry Martyn that most challenged Jimmy Graham. Suffering from increasingly worsening tuberculosis, Martyn did not even consider returning to England to convalesce. [14] He died at age 31 on a harrowing journey across Turkey to Constantinople. Though his Bible translation work was an invaluable achievement, during his lifetime he led few to salvation. However, just as God used his story to challenge Jimmy Graham to the missionary calling, so his greatest legacy may be summarized in words found in his own diary: "Even if I never should see a native converted, may God design, by my patience and continuance in the work, to encourage future missionaries."[15]

It is not completely certain that Jimmy Graham originated the following prayer, but as he grew older, it is what he prayed while contemplating God's will in his life:

"Lord, I give up all my own plans and purposes,
All my own desires and hopes,
And accept Thy will for my life.
I give myself, my life, my all
Utterly to Thee to be Thine forever.
Fill me and seal me with Thy Holy Spirit,
Use me as Thou wilt, send me where Thou wilt,
Work out Thy whole will in my life
At any cost now and forever."

Jimmy attended a fine, stately college named Hampden-Sydney, founded in 1774, southwest of Richmond. It is not particularly surprising that he attended this school. The Grahams had a long and loyal involvement with the college. In fact, some years later Jimmy's brother Tucker became one of the highly-esteemed presidents of the institution.

Upon completing his undergraduate degree at Hampden-Sydney, Jimmy Graham entered the sister school, Union Theological Seminary, for graduate study. One of his professors was a fine man of God named Thomas E. Peck. It would not be long before Peck became a mentor for Jimmy and then much more than a mentor.

It had been Peck's privilege to be taught and discipled by the great Southern preacher James Thornwell. When Daniel Webster once heard Thornwell preach, he'd raved that "it was one of the finest exhibitions of pulpit eloquence I ever heard."[16] Therefore, it was quite significant that Thornwell recommended Peck to a Baltimore church from which he himself had received a call.

Thomas Peck served as pastor of that church for about 13 years, until he was offered the professorship of church history, church government, and theology at Union Seminary. When he settled in as a professor there, it was obvious to all who knew him that he'd found his lifelong niche, and he proved it by remaining happily in that post for 33 years.

Thomas Peck was, above all, a person of integrity. He would stand immovable on principle, even voting alone if need be. To conform unabashedly to the will of God was the overarching trait of his Christian character.

A biographical sketch states that, even as a young man, he was "not fond of society, not fond of sport, but was grave and thoughtful beyond his years."[17] However, those who knew him well never viewed him as irritable or boring. He was affectionate and witty, with a laugh "so full of merriment as to be irresistibly contagious … it was a pleasure to see this grave, earnest mind abandon itself to an hilarity so free and joyful."[18]

For his dry humor and many other qualities, his family was devoted to him; his students loved him; and his friends were strongly attached to him.

Surely it was at least partly due to Dr. Peck's godly influence that Jimmy dedicated his life to service. It is not clear exactly when or how China became the spot on the planet toward which Jimmy Graham gravitated, but he became unreservedly determined to reach that field.

Almost from his first day in seminary, Jimmy had begun to notice Dr. Peck's fine collection of daughters and in time decided that one, a young lady named Sophie, was very special. As he observed her from afar, noting her outstanding qualities and her strength of character, his admiration grew. Eventually he worked up the courage to meet her, and their friendship gradually evolved into a deep and caring relationship. They began taking long walks together, but neither spoke specifically of where they surmised God might be leading them.

After many walks and many talks they finally grew bold enough to share their individual callings, learning to their delight that each had essentially a similar goal: to serve as a missionary in the Orient. It wasn't until this point that Jimmy dared ask Sophie Peck to marry him. But when he did, she accepted with the full knowledge that she was committing herself to a life of severity and danger in the then mysterious, little-traveled interior of China. The pair wasted no time. Jimmy was ordained into the ministry on July 7, 1889, and the two married in October. Within a month after the wedding he and Sophie departed for China, arriving there on December 10 of that same year.

SOPHIE PECK GRAHAM IN A
PHOTO TAKEN BETWEEN HER
WEDDING ON OCTOBER 3, 1889,
AND DEPARTURE FOR CHINA
LESS THAN A MONTH LATER.

JIMMY· (JAMES R. GRAHAM II)
WAS ORDAINED INTO
THE MINISTRY ON JULY 7, 1889,
MARRIED ON OCTOBER 3,
AND DEPARTED WITH HIS BRIDE
FOR CHINA BEFORE THE END OF
OCTOBER, ARRIVING IN
SHANGHAI ON DECEMBER 10.

"GEORGIE"
(A REPRODUCTION IN THE SIZE OF THE ORIGINAL PHOTOGRAPH)

MOST ASSUREDLY,
I SAY TO YOU,
UNLESS A GRAIN OF WHEAT FALLS
INTO THE GROUND AND DIES,
IT REMAINS ALONE;
BUT IF IT DIES,
IT PRODUCES MUCH GRAIN.

—JOHN 12:24, NKJV

CHAPTER 2

Boxers

The Grahams arrived in Shanghai during a period of relative peace 10 years before the brutality of the Boxer uprising began in 1900. The region to which they were assigned was in the northern Chinese Jiangsu province, which bordered the Grand Canal. The massive canal meandered across eastern China from Tientsin to Hangchow, linking up the Yangtze and Yellow Rivers. The longest man-made waterway in the world, it took nearly 2,400 years to build.[1] Besides becoming a vast passage for travel and trade, the canal was used for everything else too—as a reservoir, bathtub, fishing pond, and sewer.

For centuries, Jiangsu was a crucial trade center at a point where the Grand Canal joined the Huaihe and Yunyan rivers, but when the water bed elevated, it was no longer accessible by large boats, and its commercial importance waned. However, the region was heavily populated and retained an important place in Chinese history, partly because of famous individuals who had lived there, including Han Hsin, legendary general of the early Han Dynasty and several noted poets and artists.

Jimmy and Sophie Graham traveled first to Xenjiang, where they devoted themselves to a study of the Chinese language. At times an American named Rev. Woodbridge assisted them in their study. However, too often their language training consisted of sitting in a room with a Chinese who didn't know English any better than they knew Chinese. Jimmy and Sophie learned the phrase that meant, "What do you call this?" and all day long they would quiz that "teacher" until their brains felt scrambled and their tongues twisted sideways from the difficult pronunciations.

They would try out their new words on the Chinese cook on the mission station. If he stared at them in confusion and muttered dark incantations, they knew they had not learned the phrase correctly.

The typical missionary at this time would devote at least the first year totally to language study. This study was to be continued for some years with missionary duties being gradually added as the language was mastered.

During this period, Jimmy and Sophie boarded with a missionary named J.E. Bear. Bear was a devoted man of God but was constantly battling physical ailments which hindered his ministry.

In fact, years later his health was such that when it came time for the annual mission meeting in Hsuchowfu, his family urged him not to attend. His reply was, as always, "I must go about the Father's business."

First, Bear had to take a boat 130 miles down the Grand Canal to Tsingkiangpu. Most of the remainder of the journey was by mule cart, a means of transportation Jimmy considered the "most uncomfortable means of travel ever devised by man." It was a five-day trek, and by the time the party reached Hsuchowfu, Bear was prostrate with exhaustion—so wiped out that he could only attend one or two sessions. He never recovered. A few days after the conference he died quietly in his bed.

Various dialects were spoken throughout the province, but Jimmy and Sophie concentrated on Mandarin, a language that could be understood fairly well by most. Jimmy struggled long and hard to grasp the language, but Sophie seemed to catch on more quickly and became quite fluent. Throughout his ministry Jimmy's command of the language was sometimes amusingly deficient. Listeners had to use mental gymnastics to follow him, but his deep sincerity, humor, and compassion offset this weakness among the Chinese. With Sophie's knowledge of the language and her dynamic gestures and facial expressions, she eventually drew crowds of women to her Bible teaching. So though Sophie was the better speaker, what Jimmy had to preach and teach was always constructive and effective.[2]

The upper four-fifths of the Jiangsu Province was almost untouched by the Gospel with less than 100 Chinese believers among, perhaps, 30 million people. Eventually the Grahams moved to Tsingkiangpu, a town in northeastern Jiangsu with a population of approximately 130,000 (in modern China the city of Tsingkiangpu is renamed Huaiyin). Here there was a small mission station founded in 1887 by Henry M. Woods and Absalom Sydenstricker, father of Nobel Prize-winning novelist Pearl Buck. Shortly, Henry's brother Edgar, a medical doctor, joined them, as well as a woman named Miss Ellen Emerson. The Grahams arrived at the station a year and a half later.

Tsingkiangpu would undoubtedly have been unlivable were it not for a great flood levee juxtaposed against the skyline a few miles west of the city proper. It stood 125 feet high, 175 feet at the base, and about 12 feet wide. From this point it extended between 125 and 150 miles due south. This monumental embankment had been hand-built over 1,000 years before to reclaim a region immersed in water.

Like many good-sized Chinese cities and market towns in northern China, Tsingkiangpu was also surrounded by defensive bulwarks. Cities had very high, sturdy brick walls while country towns usually had earthen ones. Almost always, cities had another, larger city growing immediately outside the main wall. This might be called the suburbs, and it was usually walled also. In the early years of their work, opposition to foreigners was so bitter that missionaries could obtain no property inside the city proper, so they took whatever they could find.

Jimmy purchased a piece of land near a central connecting point called Stony Pier. There he had a flat house built with a tiled roof and at least 10 rooms. Beside it a small chapel was constructed. The Grahams did not resent being outside the main city walls. In fact, they considered living in the outer area advantageous to reach the countryside and to allow rural inhabitants easy access to them.

The couple had to become accustomed to dress and customs that seemed odd, even outlandish. Chinese women wore loose-fitting garments called *Chi Pao*, and all females except laboring, peasant women had their feet tightly bound, which resulted in pointed feet about five inches in length with arch folded, big toe extending. They hobbled, most of their weight placed on their heels.

In some ways, Chinese mothers were a bit more earthy than Western women. They would breast-feed their children publicly and would sometimes make instant baby food by chewing up peanuts or some other food and spitting it into the mouths of their infants.

The men typically wore a straight jacket, hanging loosely past the waistline, with a stand-up collar. Their pants were baggy and fastened with a wide cloth belt. Except on festival days, the predominant colors were dark blue and black.

It would be a great understatement to say that Chinese society in this era was chauvinistic. Male children received blatantly preferential treatment; female babies were sometimes allowed to die; and women were often excluded from meetings or societal privileges that men enjoyed.

The early years for the Grahams were unavoidably trying, and it can safely be said that Jimmy and Sophie were not welcomed with open arms into Chinese society. The Chinese did not want to hear of a strange new religion from these big-nosed pale foreigners—people who had routed their armies with superior weapons and who, according to local lore, collected their body parts and ground them into healing potions and changed Chinese bone marrow into gold.

Though there were no maps as such, each missionary took a different general slice of the region as his or her assignment. Jimmy, called by colleagues the "great question mark" because of his insatiable inquisitiveness, would milk dry anyone who had even a cursory knowledge of the geography, and by that means a rough map began gradually forming in his mind. The few missionaries on the station knew there was no way to cover such a vast territory by preaching town to town, so they concentrated in the early years on spreading the Gospel with written Scripture, books, tracts, and whirlwind preaching through the towns.

Travel at that time was almost entirely by wheelbarrow (predecessor to the rickshaw). The only time Jimmy mentioned riding a horse, he admitted the horse had dumped him.

"It wouldn't have been so bad getting thrown," Jimmy joked. "It was the fact that it was a Chinese horse that threw me that was so hard to swallow."

Jimmy learned to dicker with barrow-men for the fairest rate possible. In the early years he did most of the traveling. He carried his own bedding and a little extra food. The bedding was spread lengthwise inside the barrow, rolled up on one end, and he sat on it with his legs dangling on each side of the barrow wheel. Jimmy knew so little Mandarin that it was claimed that "what he didn't know about the language would fill the world and what he did know would fit easily into a thimble." However, he was so itchy for action that he'd take short trips every few months to surrounding towns, passing out tracts, and saying in tortured Chinese, "This is the Jesus doctrine." Or he'd hold out Christian books and say, "This is very good to read—it is two coppers." This is how he cut his teeth on the language—"a very painful process and hard on the teeth but never to be regretted."

The thing Jimmy liked best about wheelbarrow travel was the fact that he could disembark easily. Sometimes 10 or 15 Chinese would gather behind him as he traveled. So he would hop out of the barrow and ask their names and occupations. They would, in turn, ask him, "What is your honorable business?" or "How do you get rich?" Then Jimmy would repeat his memorized Chinese phrases about the Gospel message. He would say that all have both a soul and a body. The human body dies but, unlike the donkey or pig, the soul lives on forever. He'd remind them of the existence of heaven and hell—ideas that were not wholly unfamiliar, though the Chinese hypothesized hell to be a place 18 stories deep (the deeper, the hotter). Then Jimmy would contrast their inferior attempts to avoid hell with the way Jesus has provided.

By this time, perhaps he'd have reached the outskirts of a small village of 40 to 50 inhabitants, and several would invite Jimmy to their homes for tea. Sometimes he accepted. Other times he declined, wishing instead to continue on to a larger town where for several hours he would announce the Gospel message to people passing through the marketplaces. Many came only to see the strange light-haired, large-nosed man with too-high cheekbones. But while they stared and mumbled about the foreign devil, they always heard at least a fragment of the Gospel.

One day in a new town, he stopped at a tea house. His barrow-man, more familiar with the customs and more comfortable with the dialect, ordered tea for Jimmy. As he sat down, he overheard the other patrons discussing him.

The tea house customers did not realize Uncle Jimmy could understand Chinese better than he spoke it. After repeatedly referring to the light-skinned stranger by the commonly used derogatory term for outsiders, one of them who knew rudimentary English addressed Jimmy directly.

"Honorable guest, what is your name?"

In Chinese, Jimmy answered with one word: "Foreign."

"Ah," said the English-speaker, "and what is your honorable surname?"

Again answering in Chinese, Jimmy said "Devil." Amidst the mirth that ensued, Jimmy had new friends and a new opportunity to talk about Jesus.

If there was no tea house nearby, Jimmy would stop at a tea shop or light up his little alcohol stove, scramble some eggs, and send his barrow-man for some warm bread.

Often one Chinese onlooker would act as an authority, explaining the purpose of each article and utensil the missionary used. Of course, most of the descriptions were fantastically imaginative.

If Jimmy was carrying an American food item, occasionally an onlooker would dip a dirty finger into it for a taste, a practice Jimmy strongly discouraged. One habit the nationals found most strange was the missionaries' enjoyment of milk. The Chinese had cows, but they did not drink cow's milk and found it quite unappealing and worthless. When Jimmy pulled out his can of Borden's condensed milk, the Chinese were even more bewildered. Why would anyone take the trouble of placing cow's milk into cans?

As dusk fell Jimmy would make his way to a village inn. He'd hand out tracts and try to converse until finally, late in the evening, the crowd would disperse. Then he and the barrow-man would spread their blankets on board beds and lay themselves down for well-deserved rest. Before Jimmy fell asleep he would commit himself silently to the Father, ask a blessing for the messages of the day, and pray in particular for any especially interesting encounters. Then his eyes would open, and it would be dawn.

Instead of remaining in any town for long, Jimmy's usual strategy became one of moving quickly from town to town, teaching and passing out tracts and Gospels as he went. Then as he returned home, he would take a different route in order to systematically work a territory, and in this way new villages were constantly being touched with the Gospel.

Jimmy had a unique experience once as he entered a town. He noted several houses on the outskirts and, for some reason, began to call them his center of operations. It seemed foolish because he had no center of operations and could not begin to afford to buy the facilities. However, many years later, when the time was ripe for the mission committee to purchase a Christian school facility, they chose that town. And Jimmy was shocked to find that it was those very houses that they purchased, and Jimmy's daughter Sophie was placed in charge of the school.

At one point Jimmy traveled a circuit with a representative from the Bible Society, a Mr. Whitehouse. After about a week they came to a walled city near a waterway where a floating population of boat people also lived. Jimmy knew that boat people sometimes had a reputation as troublemakers, so he urged caution. His companion decided to sell Bibles in the town, but Jimmy wanted to preach in an adjoining area; so they parted, agreeing to meet at day's end.

At sunset, as Jimmy headed back to meet his friend, he found that even the mangy dogs on shore seemed to have turned surly. People gathered in clumps, following him up one street and down the next, calling out insults. His emotions screamed retreat, but he didn't want to abandon his Bible Society friend. One rock struck him in the back; then suddenly the air was thick with them.

Realizing the danger was escalating, Jimmy edged over against buildings and jogged next to walls in order to protect at least one side of his body. He felt a flash of pain as bamboo walloped the back of his head, but he kept running. Finally he saw the town official's home just ahead. He ducked into the man's home as more rocks clattered around him.

Instead of the sympathy he expected, Jimmy sensed only flint-hard hostility from the official.

"Other man also come into town; make trouble. He also ask for help and I provide escort out of city. No more! Not keep helping those who make trouble for himself. Go. Go on. Out of here."

Jimmy was shoved out of the house, and he ran haphazardly through the town, making sure not to get cornered. Finally he sensed he was in the suburbs. By this time blood dripped from lacerations, and his breath came in accordion-like wheezes. He knew that, above all, he must not fall. If he fell, he was as good as dead.

He wrote later, "I knew I could not stand the strafing I was getting much longer and I kept asking God to send the men away before I fell. And in a most miraculous way, He did so. Without any visible reason the mob began to drop away."

Jimmy could hear the angry voices fade. Finally, glancing behind, he saw only the village mongrels as they turned back victoriously. He collapsed by the side of the road, thoroughly exhausted. His barrow-man had disappeared long before, and he prayed desperately that somehow he'd be able to locate the man. Shortly a figure appeared about a mile away, and as he drew closer, Jimmy realized it was the barrow-man. As the man approached, Jimmy was praying fervently about what to do next. Circling the town, they looked desperately for the others in their party. Everything in Jimmy wanted to retreat immediately for Tsingkiangpu, and his barrow-man argued vehemently in favor of the idea. But against his better judgment, Jimmy waited at an inn on the outskirts of the city. Two hours passed, three, four—then miraculously, one by one, the other barrow-men, the helpers, and his Bible Society friend arrived unbidden at the same inn.

Days later Jimmy arrived back in Tsingkiangpu. Sophie saw him from a very great distance and began preparing a hot bath and readying disinfectant and gauze for his wounds.

When he limped into the house, he voiced no bitter complaints, and though sympathy shone in his wife's eyes, she said nothing that would fuel self-pity. She helped him undress, and he eased his aching body into the bath water. Every part of his body seemed covered with bruises or lacerations.

Of these early days Jimmy wrote, "One never knew just what trouble would develop, and it was liable to be very serious at times. ... It showed me what I think is true about human nature—when we know we cannot do anything ourselves we can leave it all to God and be quiet and peaceful. However, when we ... think of ourselves, rather than of God as being the one responsible for the care of others, we start to worry."

Often as Jimmy left for an evangelistic foray, he honestly did not know if he'd see Sophie again in the flesh. Early on, he had imagined that perhaps his wife was so tough that the beatings and stonings didn't bother her too much. But once, shortly after leaving for a trip, he returned for something he forgot. As he strode into the house, he found Sophie rocking their new baby, Georgia, in her arms, sobbing quietly. When she glimpsed him, she tried to hide the tears, like a child caught with fingers in the cookie jar. She'd been all smiles when he left, but now Jimmy knew the true wrenching of her heart for him. "It was there," said Jimmy later, "that God showed His great tenderness for me."

In spite of the threat, Jimmy always departed again to search out new villages. After learning what a flying rock could do even to a solid head like his, he sometimes wore a sort of hardhat. In one case he was cornered by a mob while his barrow-man, returning from an errand, hesitated and watched from a distance. Finally the barrage of stones rendered the hat useless, and Jimmy was knocked unconscious. Apparently thinking him dead, the crowd dispersed. At that point, the ever-courageous barrow-man approached, revived him a little, pulled him into the wheelbarrow, and headed toward Tsingkiangpu and Sophie.

How often did Sophie want to tell him not to travel into danger, that there were plenty of Chinese to reach just outside their back door? But each time he made new plans, she kept her silence and prayed and watched as he disappeared again in the swirling dust.

Georgia (whom they called Georgie) was their greatest delight in those days. It was the same child who had cooed and clapped at the ugly mob in the incident that opens this book. Immediately when the crowd had spied the happy baby, their mood had changed. A few began to wave and smile. As the group dispersed, the instigators goaded the rest to charge the house, but a company of soldiers rounded the corner, and the troublemakers fled.

Before she was four years old, Georgie became ill with dysentery, but the antibiotics so common today were simply not available. Though Jimmy and Sophie tried everything they knew, they could not save her life. She died on the 4th of July, 1894, with no inkling that she had very possibly saved the life of her parents. In fact, the grieving Sophie said that it seemed to her that God had sent that dear little child to break down prejudice and soften the hearts of the Chinese people.

Georgie was the first person buried in the Christian cemetery at Tsingkiangpu.

Because the evolving political conditions in China had profound implications for missionaries, it is important to understand the historical context. For several hundred years the Ch'ing dynasty had reigned in China. Throughout the 19th century, Ch'ing emperors had watched as foreigners encroached increasingly upon their land. Foreign regiments with their modern weapons were able to humble larger Chinese armies. The Opium Wars of 1839–42 between Britain and China forced China to open coastal and, later, international ports to foreign trade. The Sino-Japanese War of 1894–95 between China and Japan shamed China militarily, and the conditions of surrender deprived her of rights over Korea and Taiwan. Several European nations even began claiming exclusive trading rights to various regions in China.[3]

During the 1890s, just after the Grahams arrived in China, Emperors Kuang-Hsu and Kang Yowei attempted to strengthen the empire against foreign imperialism. The resultant outbreak of rioting by the *literati* in 1891, and again in 1895, resulted in the death of a number of missionaries. But this was just a small omen of things to come.

Shortly before the turn of the century a successful coup planned by the empress dowager, Tz'u Hsi, tore China from Kuang-Hsu's grasp. Initially she seemed to oppose violence against foreigners, but as she sensed growing Chinese resentment to international domination, she also began exploring ways of ridding her empire of "foreign parasites."

At the same time, Americans were hoping to get in on the trading bonanza. John Hay, U.S. Secretary of State, suggested what he called an "Open Door" policy which would guarantee equal trading rights for all with no discrimination. Other nations said the policy was unenforceable, but since there was no direct rejection, Hay declared it final and definitive.

At about the end of the Grahams' first decade as missionaries, Tz'u Hsi wrote a bristling letter to all Chinese provinces urging them not to make peace with the trespassers. When the starving citizens of northern Shandung Province received the missive, it lit a fuse of resentment against foreigners, whom they perceived as gaining wealth at their expense. In 1900 they initiated a secret society known as the Fists of Righteous Harmony. Outsiders eventually began calling them Boxers because they practiced martial arts.

Initially the Boxers thought they had a magical power and that foreign bullets couldn't harm them, so they brashly roamed the country, destroying Christian mission stations and slaughtering foreign businessmen, missionaries, and Chinese Christian converts. At first the Boxers feared the Ch'ing dynasty would stand against the violence, but government policy suddenly, horrifyingly changed.[4] According to the book *Beyond the Stone Arches,* by Edward Bliss, Jr., "The imperial government began offering a bounty on the heads of all foreigners, young and old. The head of a child brought thirty taels, or about twenty-two dollars. Adult heads were worth slightly more."[5]

Orders circulated from the American Consul that all missionaries were to proceed quickly to places of safety. As many as possible were to go to Shanghai or Peking. The rest were to go to their provincial capitals and seek political asylum from the governor of the province until things calmed.

James and Sophie Graham, affectionately known to fellow missionaries as "Uncle Jimmy" and "Aunt Sophie," had now lived in Tsingkiangpu for years. Uncle Jimmy hurried Sophie and their children down to Shanghai. There, reports arrived daily of a missionary killed here, a family there, and faithful Chinese Christians brutally murdered by the Boxers in other towns.

The missionaries gathered in safety lived from report to report with heavy hearts. Eventually, the totals began coming in: 30,000 Chinese Catholics and 45 Catholic church officials slaughtered. And of Protestants, 1,900 Chinese believers, 134 missionaries, and 52 of their children killed.[6]

Uncle Jimmy wondered about his friend at the Bible Society, Mr. Whitehouse, and his young bride of two weeks. They had been in Shansi Province. Were they safe?

Then came the blackest days of all. Between 46 and 100 missionaries from the northern provinces had sought refuge in the governor's courtyard at the provincial capital, Taiyuanfu, in Shansi. They did not know the governor despised all foreigners. Nor did they know that the governor himself was a leader of the Boxer uprising. Fooling the missionaries with a false show of sympathy, he gathered them together one afternoon and executed them all. Whitehouse and his bride were among them.

The question "why?" trembled on the lips of more than one brave missionary. The need had been so great, and now this waste. Numb with grief, they awaited details. But the only news was filtered by word of mouth from someone who had been told by someone who had been told by someone.

Weeks scarred with violence came and went. Finally, 20,000 Boxers advanced on the imperial "Forbidden City," just outside of which, in Beijing, lived hundreds of foreign diplomats with their families, staffs, and a small entourage of military personnel. The Boxers appeared in a frightening mass, advancing on them waving red and white standards and brandishing swords, with a deafening roar of gongs, drums, horns, and rabid yelling.

For two awful months the foreigners, with a scanty collection of firearms, held off the Boxers. But now 76 of the defenders lay dead and many more wounded. They prepared for the final, overpowering charge of the Boxers and readied themselves to die.

Then the foreigners heard several loud explosions and glimpsed a column of armed men. It was an international force sent to their rescue. Soldiers and sailors from eight countries had combined, forming a brigade 2,500 strong. With their superior weapons, they defeated the Boxers.

Jimmy Graham's rudimentary medical training was put to good use among the wounded Chinese after the "Allied Force of the Eight Nations" left the area. A few Chinese were perhaps beginning to realize the falseness of rumors picturing missionaries as demons who ground Oriental hearts and eyes into Western medicine.

Gradually the fury of the storm spent itself, and in the grim stillness that followed, Jimmy Graham returned alone to Tsingkiangpu, nearly 300 miles north on the Grand Canal, to see if it was safe enough for the others to return.

Shortly after his arrival Graham had a visitor. Few stopped to notice the stranger making his way down the narrow streets, carefully avoiding the puddles. It was night, and lamps had been lit in the little shops. Rickshaws and wheelbarrows, dogs and people were everywhere. At a little tea shop overlooking the canal, the visitor stopped a man on the street.

"Is there a foreigner living in this town?"

"No," said the man. "He took his family to Shanghai when the trouble broke out."

Someone else spoke up. "The foreigner returned a few days ago, alone. He lives up the street a little way—turn here, turn there. At the end of the little alley is a gate."

"Bang loudly," suggested another. "The gateman is deaf."

The stranger thanked them and moved on, leaving those at the tea shop to speculate: *From his speech, most likely he is from the north, where much killing took place—very dangerous.* Then they went back to sucking in their boiling tea.

"Coming," mumbled the gateman, pulling on his jacket and shuffling out of his room. Then louder, as the knocking continued insistently, "Coming! Coming! Who it is?"

He received no reply. An imperious voice demanded, "Open the gate!" He slid back the heavy wooden bolt and peered through the crack. "Who it is?"

"Is the foreigner at home?"

"Wait a minute …"

Bolting the door in the stranger's face, the gateman hurried within.

"I do not like his looks. He has an evil face," he informed Graham. "I do not like his way. He is from the north. If you tell me, I will say it is late and you do not wish to be disturbed."

"No," the missionary said. "Let him in and pour some tea."

Grumbling, the gateman obeyed. Shortly he ushered the stranger into the simple living quarters. He was an ordinary-looking man with an extraordinarily hard face. In spite of his authoritative bearing, he appeared nervous. The preliminary greetings over, he inquired what lay behind the door to the right.

"The bedroom," replied Graham.

"What lies in there?" he asked, pointing his chin to the adjoining door.

"The kitchen."

"What is in there?" his chin jerked toward the next door.

"Just a minute," said the missionary, beginning to feel irritated. "This is my home and you are my guest. It is none of your affair what lies beyond these doors."

Hastily the stranger apologized for his rudeness, adding that he was only wanting to make sure they were alone as he had some business of a very private nature to discuss. Once assured they were absolutely alone, he proceeded.

"Do you remember the foreigners who sought protection at Taiyuanfu with Yu Hsien, governor of Shansi Province?"

"I have heard."

"You have heard." The stranger fell silent for a few minutes. "I was there," he added.

"You saw them die?"

"I am captain of Yu Hsien's bodyguard. I was in charge."

"You were responsible?" But something in the man's face—so hard, so hopeless—stopped Jimmy. He could have told him what he thought. He could have lashed out at him with all the grief and indignation in him. But something sealed his lips and kept him silently waiting for the captain to proceed.

"I was following instructions," he continued. "To me, at the time, it was nothing. I am a man accustomed to killing. Another life—ten, twenty, one hundred. It was nothing.

"Yu Hsien, governor of the Shansi Province—he does not like foreigners. He does not like them, nor their ways, nor their doctrine. When they began to gather at his door asking for protection in the name of their government, his soul rankled within him. 'Protection? I can only protect you by putting you in the prison,' he replied harshly.

"So he put them in prison. For several days he kept them there while his hatred grew. Then he called me in and gave me my orders. I am a man trained to obey. I am a man accustomed to killing. These foreigners—I cared not one way or the other."

Graham flinched and shook his head.

"We led them out into the prison courtyard and lined them up. Yu Hsien was there and berated them loudly and angrily. 'I do not like you foreigners,' he shouted. 'I do not like you, or your ways, or your foreign teaching.' Then he told them they were all to be killed."

The stranger paused again—struggling for words. The missionary was sitting forward, scarcely breathing. "Go on. Go on," he whispered. "What happened next?"

"Then happened the strangest sight I have ever witnessed. There was no fear. Husbands and wives turned and kissed one another. When the little children, sensing something terrible about to happen, began to cry, their parents put their arms about them and spoke to them of 'Yiesu' while pointing up to the heavens and smiling.

"Then they turned to face their executioners, calmly as though this thing did not concern them. They began singing, and singing they died. When I saw how they faced death," he hurried on, "I knew this 'Yiesu' of whom they spoke was truly God.

"But tell me. Can God forgive my so-great sin?"

Graham thought of his close friend, Whitehouse, and his bride of a few weeks, who had been among those killed. He thought of others and felt the anger.

The captain was speaking again. "I am at present on my way escorting Yu Hsien's wife to the northeast. Tonight we rest in this city. Tomorrow we continue our journey. I sought you out, foreigner, to ask you—is there nothing, nothing I might do to atone for my wrong? Is there nothing?"

A hand was on Graham's heart as he thought to himself: *Can God forgive? What of Christ on the cross praying, "Father, forgive"? What of Saul of Tarsus, who kept the clothes of those who stoned young Stephen and persecuted those of the Way beyond measure? What of him?*

The officer sat silent, waiting. The missionary reached for his worn Chinese Bible. "Listen," he found himself saying, "our God, whom we serve, is a merciful God. True, your sin was great. Very great. But His mercy is even greater. This Yiesu is His Son who came to earth to die for sinners like you. I, too, am a sinner. All men are sinners. And because Yiesu died for you—for this Son's sake—God can forgive you."

The captain listened closely. Foreign words these, to a mind schooled to hate and to kill but not to forgive. He drank in every strange word. "Love … Forgiveness … Life." He listened. The little he could understand, he accepted simply, asking an occasional question and again listening closely.

It was late when the conversation ended and Graham escorted the captain to the gate, bowing farewell. It was the last he saw or heard of him.

Uncle Jimmy sat for a long while afterward, thinking. Fresh in his mind were hundreds of new graves strewn across China like wheat sown at random. No more the anguished "Lord, why this great waste?"

A new harvest had begun.[7]

9003—Company of Boxers, Tien-Tsin, China.

MORE THAN 30,000 CHINESE CHRISTIANS ALONG WITH MANY
MISSIONARIES WERE KILLED DURING THE ANTI-WESTERN AND
ANTI-CHRISTIAN FERVOR OF THE BOXER UPRISING, OFTEN WITH
COVERT SUPPORT OF REGIONAL OFFICIALS SUCH AS YU HSIEN,
GOVERNOR OF SHANSI PROVINCE.

Jimmy & Sophie's son, James R. Graham III
(right), with a friend.

AWAY FROM THE CANALS, WHEELBARROWS WERE THE TAXI AND FREIGHT
SERVICE OF THE DAY. THIS TURN-OF-THE-CENTURY POSTCARD FROM THE
PRESBYTERIAN COMMITTEE OF PUBLICATIONS DEPICTS UNCLE JIMMY
SETTING OUT ON AN EVANGELISTIC ITINERARY.

An attractive,
elderly Chinese lady was invited
to one of Sophie Graham's Bible studies.
After listening attentively,
she turned to a friend and said,
"No wonder they come so far across the sea
to tell us such things as these."

And how can they hear about him
unless someone tells them?
And how will anyone go and tell them
without being sent?

— Romans 10:14–15, NLT

C H A P T E R 3

HARVEST

The spiritual harvest multiplied. In fact, it grew to the point that the Southern Presbyterian Mission developed eight mission outstations, stretching into an immensely long, thin line across northern China, with over 600 miles in some cases between stations. Near the turn of the century, mission leaders decided to divide the stations into two separate regions according to dialect, location, and method of travel. With the Yangtze River the rough dividing line, the mid-China field was established to the south of the river and the North Jiangsu, above it. The four outstations in North Jiangsu spanned an enormous area populated by eight to nine million people—a daunting field to the small missionary staff.

Following the death of little Georgie, the Grahams had added three children to the family: Fanny, Sophie, and James III. The children remained at home for some years. Then, following a furlough, Fanny and Sophie stayed in America in the care of relatives and attended school there. James returned with his parents to China and attended the American School in Shanghai.

Much of the Grahams' ministry in these early decades took the form of country evangelism and administrating Chinese schools and orphanages. In 1901 Jimmy accepted the vice principalship of the Yuan Chiang Elementary School which had been founded by missionary Tai Tehming. Then with another missionary, Jimmy purchased several small houses at Sanmenlou and established an additional Christian school, the Chingyeh Middle School. Then Aiteh Women's School was founded, and Jimmy assumed leadership of both the middle school and the school for women. As the years passed, a few Chinese began to warm to this American couple who, despite bitter treatment, had now lived among them for so long.

Located north of Tsingkiangpu (Huaiyin) was Muyang, a flood corridor since ancient times. The Yellow River has changed course often over the centuries, sometimes radically. Ever since a dramatic flood altered the entire river system, including the direction of the Huaihe River, the people of Muyang have experienced some level of flooding nine out of every 10 years. Whenever a flood has occurred, it has overflowed farmland, floated homes away, even destroyed entire cities.[1]

The flood of 1906 was acknowledged to be one of the worst, even by Chinese who fought floods on a regular basis. Between the summer and the fall it rained continuously for 70 days. The flooding spread a great distance, extending up the Huaihe River toward northern Jiangsu. The entire plain became a swamp, and all crops were washed away. Food prices rocketed, and refugees from the coastal counties of Hai, Kan, Mu, Kuan, and Lian swarmed to Tsingkiangpu and the Huaiyin area. Between June and August, 600,000 homeless people settled in the northern sections of Huaiyin.

On behalf of the Chinese and Foreign Relief Association, Jimmy took charge of the organization of relief. His staff loaded mass quantities of donated rice and other grains on traditional pushcarts. Refugees formed endless lines in front of the carts, holding out the lower portion of their gowns as sacks. The staff poured allotments of grain into the gowns, and recipients would hurry home, anxious that no one steal the precious food.

In the Grahams' house stood 20 sewing machines with a seamstress at each one. They sewed and mended refugees' clothing free of charge. Snatches of cloth were also donated. These would be sewn into makeshift clothing and passed out to the most needy.[2] The love and sacrificial service offered by the missionaries during this famine profoundly affected the attitude of the Chinese in the region toward foreigners.

However, in spite of the assistance approximately 30,000 died of the cold that winter and of the plague the following spring. The human and financial losses resulting from the famine were so crushing that many children were left on their own. A British lady given the Chinese name "Miss Mu" had established an orphanage on Chilung Alley. One of the challenges the Grahams took on when Miss Mu returned to England was the management of this orphanage.[3]

Uncle Jimmy wrote home: "I doubt very much if any of you ever saw such a concentrated mass of misery and wretchedness as these children when they came to us those first days. Many of them were practically naked, many mere skeletons covered with sores from head to foot. Until one got used to it, tears were much nearer the surface than smiles. They were such a pitiable-looking bunch … stunted in growth and full of malaria and other common diseases."

First, they were nearly parboiled, then entirely re-clothed, given comfortable sleeping quarters, fed simple, wholesome food, coached to take care of themselves, and taught the elements of education. Sometimes, after a few years, relatives or friends who had rebounded a bit financially came to claim children. Other children proved untrainable and ran away to the lawless wanderlust of the street. A large proportion stayed on and got all the training the missionaries could offer. They were taught music, a trade, and much from the Bible. Quite a few gave good account of themselves as they reached adulthood.

On the political front a medical doctor named Sun Yat-sen was evolving into a revolutionary. His consuming goal became to overthrow the Ch'ing dynasty and replace it with a stable republic. After an aborted revolt in 1895, he fled China. While traveling abroad he made an intensive study of Western social and political theory and of the writings of individuals such as Karl Marx and Henry George.

In 1905 he organized a revolutionary league and gradually solidified his political aspirations. Revolution erupted again in China in 1910, and Yat-sen was elected provisional president, a position which he quickly handed over to a leader named Yuan Shih-kai. Yuan proved to be overly dictatorial, so in time Sun moved to overthrow him. The struggle for power raged, and when the dust settled in 1921, Yat-sen was the self-proclaimed president of China. He soon established the Whampoa Military Academy to train an army designed to subdue northern China. A rising star named Chiang Kai-shek became the academy's commandant. Missionaries waited and watched closely to see what implications the power struggles may have for them.[4]

The Grahams took a much-needed furlough in 1915 and visited James III, who was attending college in Virginia. They had not seen daughters Fanny and Sophie for eight long years. In fact, the girls played a trick on old dad. When he appeared on campus, Sophie escorted Fanny to meet him, introducing her as a "Sally Martin."

Jimmy wrote later, "I had quite a time talking to Sally, when suddenly she rushed at me and gave me a resounding kiss. I wasn't expecting to see Fanny at that time so they took advantage of me. I probably would have recognized Sophie, though, because she hadn't changed so much."

In the fall of 1916 Jimmy and Sophie began the long trip back to China by rail and sea. The Grand Canal was in flood stage, so the final leg of the trip had to be managed by slow boat—not the most pleasant experience. Small, bedbug-infested cabins contained ledges upon which they laid thin sleeping mats. They ate bits of food stowed in their luggage. Day and night, Chinese peered curiously through windows at the foreigners. When they used the portable toilet, a curtain had to be held up to provide even a modicum of privacy.

The bank of the canal had been broken in one place to relieve the strain upon the dikes. Water flowed out in a roar that could be heard for miles, with a suction that made it unsafe to come within a mile of the break. It took nine days to travel approximately 150 miles.

The warm welcome they received from Chinese Christians when they arrived in Tsingkiangpu brought a contrasting flash of vivid recollection about their first years in China. Soon after their return Uncle Jimmy wrote down his memory of their first arrival a quarter century earlier:

"There were not a half-dozen Christians in the immense territory from Zhenjiang on the Yangtze River up to Shantung. In a population of 20 or 25 million people, ours was the only mission station and we were simply holding on here by the skin of our teeth. We could not appear on the streets without being reviled and often stoned and we traveled for weeks without meeting anyone who knew anything about Christianity. We were misunderstood, hated, threatened, and a good, sound beating was not an entirely unknown experience."

Aunt Sophie's letter to U.S. churches one month after their 1916 return from furlough included an account of restoring their house. Surely no self-respecting American woman would have put up with it.

None of you ever saw such mold and rust and spider webs. Not only was the floor rotted but also the beams upon which the floor was laid. Carpenters had to replace every board. Water was needed for cleaning but the only water available was from the Grand Canal, so boys were given buckets to haul it. Tinners had to repair overflowing gutters and leaking buckets and water tins. Masons had to shore up sagging walls and replace broken bricks and mortar. Shavings, rotten planks, furniture, tents, stoves and much more were piled about the house. All cooking had to be done outside for many days. It was as if we'd been gone at least fifty years!

Sophie's letter also contained a number of specific victories they "came home" to. She wrote of one attractive elderly lady who was invited as a visitor to a Sunday Bible study. After listening very attentively to the study, the woman turned to a friend and said, "No wonder they come so far across the sea to tell us such things as these."

Another woman was brought to the mission station by an orphan boy who'd been converted. She told a pitiful life story that appeared symptomatic of demon possession. Sophie knelt and prayed with her for protection through the power of Christ, and the woman enthusiastically repeated each sentence. She began coming to church every Sunday and even brought her brother-in-law, who also claimed to be oppressed by evil forces.

One night Aunt Sophie awakened to a terrible racket from the courtyard of the inn next door. Formerly two murders had been committed there in one night, so immediately there was a sense of foreboding. She heard wailing, cursing, and the sound of blows being struck. Sophie felt utterly helpless as she lay in bed and prayed for whoever was involved.

The following Sunday afternoon Aunt Sophie glimpsed a young woman at the service she'd not seen before. After the meeting a believer came to Sophie and implored her to help the woman. As Sophie sat down with her, she began pouring out a personal tale of rage and cursing and fearless attacks on others. It was not the usual complaint of an abusive husband but of a wife out of control—she claimed she could not control these rampages. Sophie commented that this sounded strangely like what she'd heard in an inn courtyard a few nights before. The woman's eyes opened wide; she pointed her finger to her chest and said, "It was I."

Sophie told the woman there was no hope for her unless she called on Christ. The believers gathered around and prayed earnestly for her that afternoon. In the days following, the woman began learning to read the Bible, became more peaceful and happy, and reported that her husband was amazed and pleased at the transformation.

The following year brought drought in place of the floods of the year before. In Tsingkiangpu, only half an inch of rain fell in seven months. Uncle Jimmy said he could not think about the likely famine without a panicky feeling.

"To see the suffering during a famine," he reported, "is one of the very worst experiences one can go through."

The terrified Chinese began holding idolatrous processions, begging their idols to send rain. When no rain came, they turned angry and set an idol out in a field, exposed to the winds and the full heat of the sun, as if to say: *If you won't send us rain, we'll just let you sit out here for a while and see how you like it.*

During this period Uncle Jimmy spent five weeks visiting mission outstations in the province. He entered town after town, making his way slowly down dirty streets through masses of frenzied movement—naked children, dogs snapping and barking, wandering black pigs and chickens. He might see a beggar trying to attract attention by banging his head against a wall, jabbing a knife at his wrist, or threatening people with trained snakes wound around the neck. And somehow, through the maze, wheelbarrow pushers and rickshaw pullers wove their way to destinations, and folks transported balanced loads in baskets suspended on poles.

A heavy price had been paid for the present thriving church. Years before, as he'd preached in one marketplace, people milled past yelling disrespectful comments. He'd returned to the place many times but, at best, was met with cold indifference and, at worst, cruel treatment. The revilings cut to the heart, and the missionary reported actually thinking of himself as "the scum of the earth."

Then finally a grudging respect had germinated, and people began listening. Once as Uncle Jimmy preached and passed out tracts on the street, an elderly, well-to-do doctor and druggist called to him. He said he'd read some of the tracts and wanted to hear more. He invited Jimmy into his courtyard to talk it over quietly. Jimmy later joked that he almost jumped down the man's throat in his eagerness to do so. After discussing the Bible privately for a while, the man invited a dozen or two of his friends over, and they all listened and shot questions at the missionary until their curiosity was satisfied. A few weeks later the man walked some 35 miles to talk to him again.

This is just one of the stories about which Uncle Jimmy rejoiced as he visited the believers in the town, for now the old gentleman was a church elder and his son and several others from the courtyard that day long ago were Christians.

AMERICAN MISSIONARY CHILDREN HEAD HOME BY A
TRADITIONAL CHINESE METHOD OF TRANSPORT.

MISSIONARY CHILDREN TRYING OUT THE LATEST
DEVELOPMENT IN TRANSPORTATION.

DR. AND MRS. L. NELSON BELL WITH DAUGHTERS
ROSA, RUTH, AND VIRGINIA. DR. BELL CAME TO
CHINA IN 1916.

IF I ONLY KNEW PRAYER.
I STILL DO NOT SEEM TO KNOW HOW TO PRAY.

—A NEW CHINESE CHRISTIAN,
SPEAKING TO SOPHIE GRAHAM

HOW MANY OF US
WHO HAVE LEARNED OF PRAYER
BEFORE WE COULD PRONOUNCE WORDS
STILL HAVE SO DIM AN IDEA
OF THE POWER THAT LIES THEREIN
AND HOW IT IS THE FIRE IN OUR ENGINES,
THE CIRCULATION OF OUR SPIRITUAL LIFE,
AND THE FOOD OF OUR SOULS.

—SOPHIE GRAHAM,
WRITING HOME TO CHRISTIANS IN AMERICA

CHAPTER 4

PRAYER

Meanwhile, back in the United States God was busy calling a young doctor to serve in China. L. Nelson Bell was not thinking seriously of missions at the time. In 1913, while studying at the Medical College of Virginia in Richmond, Bell signed a baseball contract with the professional Virginia League (after it was agreed that he wouldn't have to play on Sundays). Two years later the team was sold to the Baltimore Orioles.

Bell loved baseball, but at the same time he felt a tug on his heart to serve God. For weeks he fought an inner struggle. A friend asked him one day if he'd ever considered serving as a missionary doctor. A light flashed on in Bell's heart. He dropped his ambition to become a major league baseball player and began exploring possibilities for missionary medicine in mainland China.[1]

By 1916 the decision was made, and he and his new wife agreed to travel to northern Jiangsu Province of China, replacing an American doctor at the Tsingkiangpu General Hospital who had committed suicide after only a few months of service.

Following 19 days of jolting seasickness on the open sea, Nelson and Virginia Bell were met in Shanghai by Jimmy and Sophie, who were to become two of their closest friends.

Dr. Bell would later describe Jimmy as a gentle, amusing Virginian, young at heart, a good reader, a fine tennis player, a thorough evangelist, and a lover of all sorts of fun. The deep friendship of the Bells and Grahams would hold them in good stead in the stormy years to come.

At about the same time the Bells were sailing for China, Sophie Graham, Jr., who'd been attending college in the U.S., was trying to decide whether to return to China. She later wrote,

> When the time came for a definite decision for or against returning to China as a missionary, it seemed as if America had never looked more attractive, and China never more repulsive. I was painfully certain, however, that doing the Lord's will would mean China. Fear of being deliberately disobedient to the 'heavenly vision' was my only spiritual dynamic at the time, but I thank the Lord for even that. Our unsuspecting Committee of Foreign Missions sent me out in a tremendous 'grouch.' So I for one am sure that obedience (even if it is of a miserable, pouty variety) is the 'one thing needful' and that love, joy, and all other essentials will follow.

It would have been difficult for the Bells to choose a more politically chaotic period in which to arrive in China. As has been mentioned, the Manchu dynasty had become so corrupt that in 1911 it was overthrown and replaced with the "Republic of China," founded by Sun Yat-sen. He appointed warlords to govern China's 18 provinces, imagining that he could exercise control over them and their armies.

But instead of rallying behind the emperor, soldiers of the warlords fought one another for dominance. Peasants called the soldiers "official bandits" because they raped, pillaged, and murdered on the side. When "official bandits" vacated a countryside, "dirt bandits" took over. These were civilians of the "Small Knife" society who kidnapped children, either demanding exorbitant ransoms or selling the children into slavery or prostitution. If the object was ransom, notes would arrive in small bundles containing a severed ear or finger. If ransom money was not forthcoming, perhaps a hand or a foot would be sent next. Many of the Grahams' letters throughout this period reflected the great danger the bandits represented.

Climate and natural disasters also seemed to war against the missionaries. In Jiangsu, summer temperatures often soared above 105 degrees, and monsoon rains swelled the Grand Canal to flood stage, washing away peasants' mud dwellings and fields. When drought came, winds roared down from Gobi Desert, sweeping mounds of sand across vast areas and into Jiangsu, covering every surface. At other times millions of locusts tore through the land, stripping fields and gardens of their greenery.

John Pollock records the first impressions of the Bells as they entered Tsingkiangpu, the city that would become their home for the next few decades:

They passed inside a great mud wall, some twenty feet high and saw the city on either side. The canal was nearly a hundred yards wide at this point, spanned by two ancient bridges. On its southern bank, surrounded by the outer city, rose the strong gray stone walls of the original Tsingkiangpu, which means Clear Water Depot. Boatmen bargained and women argued in loud, cracked voices. Over the gates leered decapitated heads of criminals.

Then Nelson Bell saw it, a board displaying five Chinese characters, one above the other. "*Ren tse I Uen,*" Uncle Jimmie read them for him. "Benevolent Compassionate Healing Hall" or you might translate it "Love and Mercy Hospital."[2]

The 170-bed hospital where Bell was to serve was built in 1913 by Dr. James Baker Woods. When Dr. Edgar Woods (James' brother) first arrived in China in the early 1890s, no one would rent him work space. It is ironic that the only folks eventually willing to offer him rooms to practice medicine were the Buddhists. So medical missions found a first foothold on the grounds of a cooperative Buddhist temple. Because of the location, local Chinese were willing to come for treatment. When the hospital itself was built later, no Chinese would darken the doorway. Local priests had reported a rumor from Shanghai that foreign doctors performed autopsies during which they purposely mutilated dead bodies and stole organs. Finally one frigid November night, there was a panicked banging at the compound entrance. Dr. Woods peered through the gates at a large mob holding torches. They'd carried an unconscious woman a long distance using a door as a stretcher.

"Our Chinese doctors have worked on her without success and now she is dying," they said. "If you can cure her, we'll start coming to you. If not, you die and all your family."

Dr. Woods knew that if he hesitated, fear for his family would paralyze him, so he quickly steeled himself, opened the gate, and waved them in. When he examined the woman, he discovered a 34-pound fibroid tumor of the uterus. He operated, removed it, and she recovered. From that day forward, there was never any shortage of patients—after all, the woman only happened to be the mayor's wife.

So grew the reputation of Woods among the Chinese, that when Chinese bandits kidnapped the Woods' son, Russell, the senior bandit found out and flew into a rage, claiming that years before Dr. Woods had saved his life and that they would not only return Russell immediately but would always from that day on protect the Woods family.

Drs. Woods and Bell were to develop a true friendship based on affection and mutual respect. Woods was a stubborn old soul and many were the heated arguments between him and Dr. Bell, but such was their Christianity that, following an argument, they never ceased to treat each other warmly as brothers in Christ.

Dr. Bell often performed as many as nine operations in a morning, then rode a black Harley-Davidson motorcycle with sidecar on house calls. Many Chinese, however, did not trust Western doctors.

To beggars, a tumor or open sore that wasn't too painful was a distinct asset. They could attract more sympathy if they displayed it prominently to passing throngs.

Superstition or fear also caused some to mistreat their bodies or deprive themselves of care. Cases were recorded in which Chinese allowed tumors to grow to 60 or 70 pounds before they resorted to Western medicine. The record was a woman who came to Dr. Bell for surgery lugging her 94 pound abdominal tumor in a wheelbarrow ahead of her.[3]

Other ways of the Chinese left Dr. Bell scratching his head. Sometimes when a child was born, the placenta was not removed. In fact, a doctor might examine a woman some time after a birth and find a dirty old shoe attached to the cord. A superstition said that the shoe might help the placenta walk away.[4]

During this same period, Uncle Jimmy completed another circuit to the churches in his district. He reported that 500 men and women in his assigned section had been examined for baptism. Out of that number only 28 were baptized. One of the individuals baptized had been examined 13 times and most of the others, six or eight times. This may appear overly stringent to modern observers accustomed to more relaxed practices in North American churches, but it made for a much more faithful group of church members in the end.

Jimmy and the session looked for solid evidence of conversion. A convert had to be able to explain the plan of salvation and tell why he or she wished to become a member; in addition, acquaintances had to provide testimony that the individual was seeking to live the Christian lifestyle before family and neighbors.

It didn't matter how many times a person was assessed or how satisfactorily he or she could answer questions. The session had to be convinced that one's Christian character was exemplary and the reputation good before baptism would be approved.

Of course, there were gracious exceptions. Once, when Graham was exhorting about the difference between true and false believers, an elderly woman, soon to be baptized, blurted out, "Could anyone imagine that an ancient lady like me could be false? Why, if at this age I confess a false belief, I think even hell would be unwilling to accept me!"

Another old lady of 83 did not answer the session's questions very succinctly. Finally she said, "I know I am not answering the questions well. My memory is bad but I know that Jesus is my Savior and that God is the only true God and I pray to Him every day."

Uncle Jimmy answered, "Old Mother, I am going to baptize you," to which she remarked softly, "It is the grace of God."

Some of the Chinese Christians served with a special urgency. One poor farmer was the only believer in his whole area. When he learned he'd contracted a fatal disease, he came to Uncle Jimmy with tears running down his cheeks. He was not weeping because his death was imminent but because he "was going before the Father's throne," he said, "with no fruit in my hands."

A convert named Mr. Kao knew the Bible as well as he knew the Chinese classics, and he made a powerful impression wherever he went. One original Gospel parable he used to teach was about a man who fell into a deep and slimy pit.

"When he could not climb out," Mr. Kao said, "Confucius passed by, saw the man in the pit and said, 'Poor fellow, if he'd listened to my wise advice, he'd never have ended up there.' Buddha happened along, saw the man and said, 'Poor fellow, if he will come up here, I'll help him.' And he walked on. Then Jesus Christ came and said, 'Poor fellow,' and jumped down into the pit and lifted him out."[5]

When Kao learned that he had a defective heart that could quit at any moment, it only made him more earnest in his witness than before.

However, as the church grew, so did the plague of banditry. Well-armed bandits roamed the countryside in large companies, committing crime almost at will. The soldiers sent to stop the bandits were quite content to receive food, clothing, and a salary as long as they could avoid injury. At times they even seemed to be bandit allies. They'd grab some unoffending peasants working in the field, beat them, drag them into town, and report catching 10 of the bandits. Finally, when the soldiers' masquerade had become sufficiently embarrassing, officials might either force the soldiers into serious fighting or else buy off the robbers for a while.

Occasionally a warlord would get fed up and track down particular bandits for execution. In one case in Sutsien, six bandits were executed, or more accurately, mutilated to death as a deterrent to others. Their arms were cut off, their legs broken, their ears chopped off, and their eyes punched out. Then they were skinned, beheaded, and had their hearts cut out.[6] And yet the cycle of banditry and kidnapping continued.

In the midst of the chaos, Uncle Jimmy believed profoundly that Christianity was the greatest need in China and the only thing that could save her from anarchy. Some non-Christian Chinese were beginning to see the light. A dyed-in-the-wool Confucianist told him, "Your mission schools are the only ones that are teaching anything like real morality to our young men and women and it is beginning to tell on the Chinese character already."

Jimmy respected the persistent resilience of the Chinese—this people which had spent decades building the Great Wall and had hand-dug the Grand Canal, each stretching hundreds of miles across China. But he wrote of the Chinese, "They have every other quality that would make them one of the greatest nations in the earth today, but because they are throwing over true morality, they are the plaything of the nations of the world and I very much fear that it is only a question of time before they have to go under the control of some other nation until they learn their lesson."

Spiritually, his attitude reflected a joy tinged with sorrow: "Opportunities and spiritual openings which seemed an extravagant dream years ago are available to us every day and we are straining to the breaking point, limited only by dollar power and man power. And a million a month in China are dying without God."

There was a civil war raging in central China. The nation was so enormous and communications so poor that, even when people learned of crises, they didn't show much concern if it was occurring a far distance away. The peasants in Tsingkiangpu had enough to worry about in their own area. The bandits were so bold that a body of approximately 1,000 of them marched openly through the region, replete with waving flags and bands.

Attendance in the mission schools dropped off, the people being afraid for their children to leave home lest they be kidnapped. Most nights, adults held vigil with weapons in hand to repel possible attack.

Yet opportunities for evangelization were still numerous, and in a March 1918 letter, Uncle Jimmy questioned why financial support from churches in America had fallen at least a third. Reflecting the personal strain, he wrote, "Trying to make brick without straw is using up the gray matter from the inside of our heads and putting it on the outside in the shape of gray hairs."

In the same month, Aunt Sophie sent a letter to churches at

home, expressing cause for joy. She told of a Buddhist woman 72 years old, a very strict vegetarian and considered very virtuous. When the lady fell ill, her Christian daughter had much occasion to share her faith as she attended to her mother. The mother finally embraced Christ, broke her fast, destroyed her idols, and burned her Buddhist books.

Once Aunt Sophie asked her, "Why did Christ allow Himself to be crucified when He had the power to save so many people?"

The new believer answered slowly and wisely, "I think He did not save Himself because in so doing He would make it impossible to fulfill His Father's will, which was that He should come and die for the sins of the world."

Another woman commented once, "If I only knew prayer. I still do not seem to know how to pray."

Sophie replied, "Do you know who is keeping you in the dark about prayer? It is the devil—he'd rather you'd do anything rather than understand the secret and power of prayer."

Sophie wrote about this incident to Christian friends in the U.S.: "I could not help thinking of how many of us who have learned of prayer before we could pronounce words still have so dim an idea of the power that lies therein and how it is the fire in our engines, the circulation of our spiritual life, and the food of our souls."

With a conviction of the efficacy of prayer, Jimmy and Sophie reminded American Christians that they could themselves have a very personal part in bringing people in other countries to salvation.

Pick a country where you know the Gospel is being preached and "ask God to add a soul through your particular prayer," they urged, "and perhaps when you get to the 'other side' you will meet some that came to Christ because of your prayer. How you saints at home could help us with strong and unwavering prayer!"

While they sought to deprive no one of the Gospel, it intrigued and disturbed them that some seemed so open to hear and others seemed so indifferent or even hostile. Uncle Jimmy reported that he never traveled his evangelistic circuit without coming back overwhelmed with a sense of the "vast unreached multitudes through whom we must pass to get to those points where, for some providential reason, there are people who have accepted or are willing to study the gospel."

Sophie had a similar experience in which, as she sat on a millstone, four or five women stood or sat on tiny stools listening intently or running to call a relative to hear the things "so good to hear." She saw three of those women believe in Christ that very day. However, at the next village, the women were cordial and polite but showed not one spark of interest in the message. She marveled at the contrast.

As schools were built, the traditional wheelbarrow mode of
transportation evolved into a school bus. This sketch of "old
China" from a Methodist girls school in Tientsin is by Walter "Wal"
Paget (1863–1935), who was the illustrator for Robert Louis
Stevenson's *Robinson Crusoe*. The drawing is from a postcard based
on a series of Paget's drawings titled "If I Lived in China."

After the death of daughter Georgia, Jimmy & Sophie Graham had three children: James R. Graham III, Fanny, and Sophie Jr. The two girls were dog-lovers, a sentiment not shared by their brother.

BEFORE YOU CAME HERE
AND TOLD US THIS GOSPEL,
MY HEART WAS JUST TEN PARTS OF BITTERNESS.
I HAD NOT ONE RAY OF HAPPINESS,
BUT NOW I AM JUST PASTED ON TO GOD.

—A CHINESE CHRISTIAN WOMAN

CHAPTER 5

FRUIT

The civil war in northern China and the banditry made for a precarious existence filled with so much killing as to almost overwhelm.

Sophie wrote, "All of us feel the heavy burden of war on our hearts. Do not imagine we are unmindful of it. I could weep dozens of times a day for the flowing blood, breaking hearts, and terror-stricken thousands. We are ourselves in a political turmoil. Soldiers hurry from north to south and back again. Hordes of robbers go in bands of hundreds and take whole villages at a time, burning, pillaging, and stealing girls and children right off the street. One of our inquirers lost his daughter a week or two ago and can find no trace of her."

A plague had spread to Nanking and was causing great fear up and down the Yangtze. Masks were made to put on at a moment's notice. However, Aunt Sophie reported that the deaths in their area appeared to be from a meningitis-like illness rather than the pneumonic plague.

Knowing that a view of these events from a human vantage point would only bring panic and despair, at the close of her letter Aunt Sophie urged readers to try to view world problems from God's perspective:

"I should be glad to think that all of our ministers and Christians were searching into the prophets for a knowledge of God's world design as unremittingly as they devour the untrustworthy daily newspapers. But I'm very much afraid that, with many, Jeremiah, Daniel and the minor prophets and Revelation are seldom investigated and whenever we set aside any of God's revelation, we are the losers and get into sad mistakes."

Some months later Uncle Jimmy reported a lengthy lull in bandit activity. However, the thieves explained very frankly that they were only waiting for the crops to be gathered and sold so they'd be able to extort more money from their victims. With sardonic humor Jimmy said of them, "The Chinese are such a thrifty, common-sense folk."

When not traveling to visit churches, Uncle Jimmy did evangelistic work in the hospital wards and the dispensary. The chapel ministry involved preaching to masses of patients, while the ward work consisted of getting personal with individual patients. The utter spiritual famine among these people was clearly illustrated when one patient, upon hearing the name of Jesus, asked in Mandarin, "What is this Jesus thing? Do you eat it?"[1]

After 10 years of directing the Boys' Orphanage, the Grahams were in process of closing it down. The need for it was ebbing, though it had been a pleasant work with few difficulties compared to the obstacles faced in mission outstations.

In respect for the Chinese culture, Aunt Sophie worked almost solely with women. Women constantly came to her home, and she never turned them away. If she was busy, she would usher them upstairs to her bedroom and work at her desk while they conversed.

Often it was poor Chinese women who came, and sometimes they asked for money. If she had any extra money, she gave it to them freely.

Sophie took her teaching very seriously, developing handmade graphics and other visual aids. She mapped out a course of study for new believers, consisting of progression through seven or eight courses. The first few classes incorporated simple Bible verses, hymns, and prayers. Next, they walked through a primer which taught basic themes of the Christian life. Then Sophie led them into lengthier Bible passages—portions of Genesis, a few Psalms, and the gospel of John. Periodically she would visit the groups and question each member to determine if she was ready to progress to the next level. In this way, the women were eventually studying the Bible systematically on their own.

By April 1919 Aunt Sophie's work among women living at the North Gate grew to a point that some were forced to stand outside the windows to hear the Bible study. Two *Tai-Tais*—refined, intelligent women of leisure, were visited by one of Sophie's "Bible women." The woman found that, though the Tai-Tais knew nothing of Christ, they'd already come to despise idols and all the rituals the Chinese called religion. The worship of ancestors was the only belief they espoused because, in their words, it showed respect for the departed.

These two attended the very next North Gate service, and the physically stronger one began walking long distances to attend church on Sundays, Bible class on Tuesdays, evangelistic class on Wednesdays, North Gate on Thursdays, and a Bible class again on Fridays. Within six weeks this woman who knew nothing biblically was flipping to Ephesians, Colossians, Hebrews, and other books as if she'd studied the Bible all her life. She also began telling her friends and family about the religion of Christ. She taught her daughter-in-law and her slave girl how to read the Bible, and they each stood the jeers and deriding wonderfully well.

Once, the son of the family came in and saw them all reading the Bible and said sarcastically, "Oh, you are all heavenly kingdom people, are you?"

"Exactly!" they answered. "That's what we hope for and may it indeed be true."

When friends warned them that the missionaries were only after their eyes, heart, and other organs after death, they answered amusedly, "Well, if they can use those portions of our anatomy to good advantage and the healing of others, they're welcome to them."

One woman who attended the Bible studies was elderly and not well dressed or well groomed. Inadvertently Jimmy and Sophie did not spend much time with her. But three months later, when they returned to her village, the woman met them with great excitement. Without knowing how to read one character, she had memorized 10 hymns. She sang them all, beaming at certain lines that brought her special delight. She'd begged people to read the hymns over and over to her until she memorized them. She'd learned much Scripture by word of mouth, and her prayers sounded like those of a mature Christian. She could also recite the topics of each sermon Uncle Jimmy had recently preached. When asked how she'd progressed so well, she said that she always prayed to the Spirit to purify her heart and to enlighten her brain to understand more each passing day.

The outstation churches were growing well at this point, and baptisms had almost doubled from the year before. Giving had also increased significantly, though Uncle Jimmy believed that calling the typical Chinese peasant earnings an income seemed farcical. He estimated that a typical salary was about five dollars per month, yet many agreed of their own accord to tithe out of that amount.

Also, most outstations had established what they called a "Society for the Propagation of the Gospel" among their neighbors. Each church member would spend a day or two each month spreading the Gospel to neighboring villages. This was one of the brightest signs of spiritual life among the churches.

Since Sophie had developed a ministry among the women and Jimmy oversaw churches covering a vast area, the two sometimes parted for days or weeks at a time. She described the typical peasant home she visited:

"They reserve the best places for the fruits of the field. By the time harvest is gathered, there is no place left for people! We sat among great matting baskets of beans, corn, peanuts, and sweet potatoes. In one place I stayed overnight, I couldn't possibly even turn around. You can't imagine the noises I heard in the night as rats came for the corn and weasels, for the oats. I felt very thankful it was not the season for snakes."

Meanwhile, Uncle Jimmy was serving on committees to determine which believers were to be approved for baptism. About 10 years earlier one young man had earnestly inquired about Christianity. Then something happened to turn him completely against the Gospel. Finally he came back, stating that he could not get the Bible out of his mind. He now knew it was true and wished to be baptized.

An ex-army officer had been baptized six years earlier, and now his wife, three of his sons, and his daughter-in-law were uniting with the church. A woman who had formerly been demon-possessed was receiving baptism as well as the daughter of a famous ex-governor.

Uncle Jimmy thought ludicrous the claim of critics that Chinese converts were mostly "rice Christians," that is, people joining the church to gain temporal benefits. He mentioned in rebuttal individuals such as the wife of a village official in Peking. Since her conversion, the husband had been making life thoroughly miserable for her and sounding as if he may abandon her. Jimmy marveled that the woman was taking the persecution quietly and calmly, as if it was not such a hard fate.

By this point mission success in the whole province had multiplied. After 30 years of service those in the mission compounds were reaping the results. There were seven outstations equipped with boarding schools, and mission hospitals treated some 75,000 people annually. About 15 to 20 organized churches existed, with combined memberships of about 4,000 and with approximately 10,000 inquirers. There were over 100 day schools as well as boarding schools housing several hundred students.

Biblically liberal missionaries did try to confuse the Chinese regarding such doctrines as the inspiration of Scripture and the deity of Christ. Some claimed the Bible was no more inspired than any other good book and that significant parts of it should not be credited as God's Word. Others taught that Jesus was not really the son of Mary or was not the incarnated Son of God. At the Kuling missionary conference that year, a league was formed to bear witness to God's Word as inspired, to Jesus as fully God and fully man, and to salvation as coming through Christ's redeeming blood alone.

Nelson Bell continued his expansion of the hospital work, and he was gaining an unsmudged reputation not only as a skilled doctor but also as a devout man of faith. Uncle Jimmy raved about Bell. He'd shake his head and say, "That Nelson! He's the greatest fellow I ever saw. What's that new expression I read, 'go-getter'? That's what Nelson is; he's a go-getter!"

Virginia kept very busy running the Bell household, rearing children, and entertaining the many Chinese that Nelson brought home. In June 1918, Virginia had borne a daughter christened Rosa, and now two years later another daughter, Ruth, was born. It would certainly have overwhelmed the Bells if they knew then the destiny of little Ruth. Way off in a southern corner of the United States, God was even then preparing one of the great evangelists in history to marry her.

Nelson Bell was a staunch tennis enthusiast, and he played to ease the stress of multiple hours of surgery. When Uncle Jimmy wasn't itinerating, he sometimes played a match or two with Nelson.

One sweltering July afternoon he and Jimmy were playing a hard singles match, and sweat was pouring off them. A dignified Chinese gentleman looked on, hands carefully folded in the sleeves of his expensive gown.

Finally, with a bewildered expression, the man bowed and asked, "Honorable sirs, could you not hire coolies to hit ball for you?"[2]

In an April 1920 letter, Uncle Jimmy described the demanding preliminary work that preceded evangelistic meetings in a town. First, Jimmy and Sophie posted notices at each gate of the city. Then they went personally to every store and every home and left written invitations. Third, they walked to every village within reach, officially inviting each one to the host village. Along the way they invited all they met on the roads.

Sometimes as they walked, a storeowner or merchant would permit them to share the message right there. They'd haul out benches for the visiting couple, and the men would smoke their pipes in various attitudes of relaxation, asking questions and making remarks as Uncle Jimmy spoke.

On market days people within a radius of three or four miles would congregate. The following day a market would be held in a town about five to 10 miles in another direction. Passing out Gospel tracts and then preaching, Uncle Jimmy could almost always gain an audience.

One day he was asked to conduct the funeral for a poor peasant woman who'd been in the church for about 20 years. The funeral procession started at her wretched little hut and moved to the church burying ground. Only a few friends and a herd of ragamuffin children attended the funeral. They buried her as the sun set on the hills. Uncle Jimmy said it was a pitiful scene, for she had no family and almost no one to mourn for her.

But after the funeral he sat with a few other missionaries, and they spoke of the woman. She had lived her life in poverty, with its many inherent drawbacks, yet she'd retained her independence throughout and never begged for money. Though the church did help her occasionally, she responded by giving to various causes with the "widow's mite." She faithfully told others of Christ, and once when she was hospitalized, patients had constantly asked that she be allowed to come to their rooms and tell them more of the "Doctrine." A well-to-do lady claimed she'd come to salvation because of what this old woman had shared. In turn, the lady's mother, nephew, and four sisters-in-law all became Christians.

After this discussion of the old woman's life, Uncle Jimmy said that the sordid surroundings and the bare grave out in the fields suddenly appeared to take on a sort of holy halo because of the fruit of her life.

During the summer and fall of 1920, many peasants in the Grahams' region had to flee their homes for weeks at a time. The hordes of robbers were so numerous, cruel, and strong that the people hid themselves in open fields, in ditches, sometimes even behind gravestones.

There were stories of God's protection. One Christian was stopped on a road and asked his name, business, and destination. Then the armed man demanded to see what was in his backpack. Upon seeing the pile of tracts and New Testaments the man said, "That's all right, you may pass on."

A few Christians were abducted and held for ransom, redeemed only at heavy cost. One elderly believer was placed against a wall to be shot. A bandit aimed at her head, but just as he pulled the trigger, she ducked her head and the bullet zinged past. Then as he aimed at her legs, she swung them into the air and he missed again. So his fellow bandits said, "This old woman was not intended to die; we must let her go."

In early 1921, Uncle Jimmy visited the town of Matsung, a

center for about eight mission schools. Since he was holding a communion service, he invited the schoolteachers into town. When they appeared, he realized that eight of the young gentlemen were former children in the orphanages the missionaries had administered. Now they were quiet and dignified, more highly respected as men of culture and education than any others in their neighborhoods. These Christians could go into any Chinese setting and be given a position of influence. They could explain their biblical convictions and also enter any ordinary conversation and present themselves with clarity and force.

Uncle Jimmy said, "These had been just as dirty and ignorant and diseased as any of that wretched band of children. They had certainly been as unpromising soil as any I ever saw and I could not help exclaiming 'What hath God wrought!'"

Meanwhile, Sophie reported on several women who were inspiring her. In order to attend church, one old woman with a bad foot had to crawl inch by inch across a slippery curved rock bridge. The woman said, "Before you came here and told us this Gospel my heart was just ten parts of bitterness. I had not one ray of happiness, but now I am just pasted on to God."

Mrs. Giang was very unusual among Chinese women. She was an excellent reader. In fact, she'd studied the New Testament until she was perfectly familiar with the life of Christ and much more. Sophie reported in a letter to U.S. friends that the woman would love to begin teaching the Bible but her husband, according to Sophie, was "proud as Lucifer and, as he belongs to an old family and has a big name to sustain, he can't belong to the 'foreign devil' clan." He told his wife to go ahead and read and study the Bible, that it would make her a good woman, but he couldn't consent to her being baptized. Sophie continued, "I want you to break his backbone of pride with your prayers. I do want to see him a different man when we go out there again."

A Mrs. Gao at Ma Tsang, the Grahams' most northern

outstation, was one of the illiterates. She was trying desperately to read a little Gospel book Sophie had given her. When Sophie visited the station, the woman said she kept forgetting the Chinese characters. "So," she exclaimed, "when I cannot think it up, I just get down on my knees and beseech the Holy Spirit to quicken my memory and make me remember, and He does!" This woman, with her modest smattering of Bible knowledge, was already trying to teach her husband, son, daughter-in-law, and other young ladies in the neighborhood.

Uncle Jimmy once stated that the most heartbreaking burden for the missionaries was the realization of all that they were *unable* to accomplish. This, he believed, tended to break men down out in the field. It was this fact and the remark of one of his assistants that motivated him to arrange for a revival period for all the church leaders from the stations. The assistant had said that he got extremely lonely for lack of touch with fellow-leaders—that he was 'giving out' all the time and never replenishing his spiritual knowledge and energy.

Uncle Jimmy arranged for workers from many miles around to come together quarterly for reports of their work, Bible study, and prayer. Leaders described personal struggles, ministry problems, encouragements, and prayer needs. Wisely, he arranged that all the preaching and Bible study classes were conducted by the Chinese leaders themselves.

Many attenders of these quarterly meetings impressed Uncle Jimmy, but he described one in particular. He was an older man than the others, nearly 60 years of age. Before he was converted, he was a dyed-in-the-wool Confucianist and idolater and, like most Chinese, a great gambler. As he matured in the faith, he was made an elder and eventually a preacher. With his fine gifts as a speaker, his thorough knowledge of the Bible, and his command of the Chinese classics, he often made a powerful impact on educated or old-style Chinese audiences. Uncle Jimmy liked nothing better than to introduce to him a stolid Confucianist who'd heard the Gospel but still clung to his old beliefs.

"I sit by," said Uncle Jimmy, "and divide my time between smacking my lips over the fine and convincing way he goes about his job and prayer that it may have the result we both long for. It is a fascinating thing to hear him expounding some incident, parable, or other scriptural passage from the Oriental point of view. This point of view has changed my outlook on many passages in the Scriptures."

While staying temporarily in Kiangyin, Aunt Sophie was asked by one of her Bible assistants to teach a Bible course some had been unable to attend when she'd taught it previously. Several other women heard of it and said they wished to attend. Then the brother of Mrs. Yang (another Bible assistant) asked if he could come sit by the door. Though it was a women's class, Aunt Sophie knew the man was dying of advanced tuberculosis and was a "splendid fellow," so she gave him approval. Then Mr. Sin, one of Uncle Jimmy's assistants, began to listen outside the window with a Mr. Yang. Then a teacher from the government school came to the window, then another missionary assistant, and finally the son of one of Sophie's "Bible women." It was an unusual mixture for a Chinese Bible class, but she taught them until the day she had to begin her circuit to outstation churches again.

During this period Aunt Sophie met a very aristocratic elderly lady. She'd been a devout Buddhist for decades and had accumulated no end of merit in herself. When given a Bible, she read and announced that it was good. But, in a quandary, she decided she would believe in both Buddhism and Christianity. Sophie said she must choose one and pointed her to the cross, the God-man dying for the world.

"If you look lightly on this and turn your back upon it," Sophie said, "you've doomed yourself forever, for God has no other Son that He will send to redeem us fallen men, and do not think there is any other way under heaven."

Mrs. Wu, one of Sophie's Bible women, came to her and said she was going for one last visit to the old lady. If she rejected Christ, it would be the final visit.

Late that evening, Mrs. Wu returned with delight shining from every pore. After a great battle, the woman had decided to give up her old ideas and wished to be baptized in the spring.

Uncle Jimmy proved again what unusual functions missionaries are sometimes called upon to fill. A 22-year-old Christian approached him and said he thought it about time he was betrothed. Jimmy agreed and asked who he had in mind. The man said he had no idea—that whomever Uncle Jimmy suggested would be okay. The young man was educated and known as "a nice young fellow," so Jimmy mentioned the names of several young ladies who had recently graduated from the mission school. The suitor had never spoken to any of them, but after a little thought, he picked one out. Uncle Jimmy said he didn't know if she'd be willing but that he'd do his best for the young man.

"It is not important," said the suitor stoically. "If she is unwilling, you can try another one."

Jimmy realized he'd only courted one woman and it had taken a good many years to convince her to accompany him in life, so he did not approach his task with an overwhelming sense of confidence. But he thought that, if his mediation yielded a marriage similar to his own, the young man would eventually have cause to rise up and call him blessed.

The long and short of it is that the first young woman had just agreed to marry another man. Uncle Jimmy contacted his friend and broke the news gently. The suitor did not even blink an eye. He only said, *"Puh yao ging,"* which means, "It doesn't make any difference," and began to discuss one of the other girls.

Uncle Jimmy went to the next girl, and she also turned him down promptly and decisively, stating that she was too young to marry and she didn't want to anyway. He tried harder, bringing up all the good traits and qualities of the man, but she stood firm. Jimmy felt slightly sick at the prospect that the third young lady may respond in the same way, and he realized that any enthusiasm he'd possessed for matchmaking had mysteriously vanished.

He even told how the story ended, but it was quite obvious that the suitor sensed significantly less anguish over the situation than did tender-hearted Uncle Jimmy.

Aunt Sophie Graham   Uncle Jimmy Graham

The Grahams' home in Tsingkiangpu, shown in a photograph taken in the late 1980s. The building has been expanded and refurbished by a local church for use as an eye clinic serving the poor.

You can have a very personal part
in bringing people in other countries to salvation.
Pick a country where you know
the Gospel is being preached
and "ask God to add a soul
through your particular prayer,
and perhaps when you get to the 'other side'
you will meet some that came to Christ
because of your prayer.
How you saints at home could help us
with strong and unwavering prayer!"

—Jimmy and Sophie Graham

CHAPTER 6

BANDITS

The summer of 1921 brought massive flooding in both northern and southern China. When the torrents began, Sophie, on one of her itinerating trips, was stranded out in the middle of nowhere. The only positive side of the situation was that she had plenty of time to write home to churches in the U.S.

She told of scorpions in abundance. One had just been spotted crawling down the partition of the room in which she sat. However, she knew that if she stopped itinerating, it would in no way rid her of the poisonous creatures. She claimed with pride that she'd personally caught and disposed of two perfectly huge ones in her own house before leaving on the trip. She actually came within an inch of taking one up in her hand, thinking in the dim light that it was something else.

The Bradleys, another missionary family, had recently come to the area. "Bandits climbed aboard their boat," wrote Sophie, "and discussed which of the children they would steal away. But God

87

influenced their minds and made them decide that the time to take the foreigners had not yet come."

Moving to the subject of recent conversions, Sophie exulted over a fired-up new Chinese Christian who had already brought in 10 Gospel inquirers, all of whom had since endured persecution. A sorceress had embraced Christ, gathered together all her instruments of divining, and thrown them into the river. It was a very brave act, and the woman admitted a great fear that an evil spirit might now inflict her with the black measles. Sophie challenged the woman not to worship the spirit, build houses for it, or burn incense to it. "Be very courageous," Sophie told her, "and if the evil spirit comes after you, call to it and tell it you are not afraid."

Uncle Jimmy was busy with a group of Chinese elders, examining candidates for ordination. The Chinese were taking another small step toward becoming indigenous. He noticed that they joined more freely than ever in the ordination discussions and candidate questioning. Within a few years they would perhaps be able to stand on their own.

The elders decided to call roll at every single session. Then, to cap it off, roll would be called one last time before they adjourned late in the night. Inevitably, some failed to answer the final call, and all one heard when their names were called was a gentle snoring.

While returning from a trip in April 1922, Uncle Jimmy saw one of the saddest things he'd ever seen in this nation of sad sights. He heard the beating of a gong and spied a religious procession. There were flags and lanterns carried by boys, then an incense table balanced by a raggedly dressed man. Then followed the idolatrous chair in which an idol is placed and transported through the streets. The usual gaggle of people trailing behind was not orderly. They stumbled along with sticks in one hand and a long rope or bamboo pole in the other. Every member of the procession, except a few in the lead, was completely blind. Most were beggars dressed in tatters, carrying only the dirty earthen bowls in which they received scraps of food or small coins. As a guild they were going to the temple to pray that they'd be protected from the greed and cruel treatment of people with good eyes and the good things of life. It was sickening to see the earnestness with which they trusted for protection in an idol made of dried mud. The scene affected Uncle Jimmy so powerfully, he remarked that if the friend of Bartimaeus had been there, the hopeless individuals would certainly have encountered a word of healing from His infinitely caring heart.

That spring Uncle Jimmy and Sophie had opportunity to see both their son and their daughter, though for very different reasons. Their son, James III, and his wife, Louise, arrived in Tsingkiangpu for language study, in preparation for a missionary career in China. James did not actually need the study, having learned the Chinese language from infancy, but his wife was starting from scratch.

Daughter Sophie Jr. had developed appendicitis, and mom went to Shanghai to be with her through the surgery, from which she recovered well.

There may have been some level of confusion among missionaries during this period as to the exact definition of *culturally indigenous*. A letter from Aunt Sophie seems to reflect this. In apparent reaction against adapting church practice to the Chinese culture, she wrote, "It seems to me one of the glories of Christ's church has ever been that it was suited to the very needs it was meant to supply of every people, tribe, and nation. I have yet to see any really converted Chinese who felt there was any change necessary to make the church suited to him or her."

In the next paragraph she brought in higher criticism and added, "There is much talk these days about suiting the preaching and teaching of God's Word to the present time, present demands, modern thought and science, etc., and it makes one tremble with apprehension, for when man begins to improve on God's ways, there is a crash coming as sure as that next winter is coming and surer. If there was ever a time to be anchored in God's Word, it is now."

It seems that Aunt Sophie may have associated indigenity with theological liberalism. She may also have been tempted to identify American church traditions and methodology with the unchangeable ways of God. However, as Jimmy and Sophie taught and trained Chinese to be leaders and pastors, they increasingly left the shepherding and teaching of local churches to these leaders. They also respected Chinese customs, learning how to approach varied situations without offense. Perhaps without being fully aware of it, they were doing a skillfully efficient job of building a culturally indigenous church in the biblically conservative sense.

The floods of 1921 had left much of the territory underwater nearly until Christmas. Now famine was rampant. The Grahams and other missionaries distributed funds for food and oversaw the repair work of canal digging and road making around the mission outstations.

In spite of the hazards, the spiritual dividends were significant in the Grahams' area. During the year, 124 adults were baptized. This was nearly 30 more adults than had ever before been baptized in a year. Now, in the whole North Jiangsu Mission there were between 5,600 and 6,000 church members. This was cause to rejoice. Five years before, after 25 years of work, there were 2,600 members. When the Grahams started their missionary service, there had been considerably less than 100.

On the other side of the coin, more church members had to be expelled from membership on this year than ever before. Uncle Jimmy wrote, "It is much better to get rid of the dead wood … than to have them in the 'fold' infecting the other sheep with their coldness and unbelief."

Sometimes hard decisions had to be made. A merchant friend of Uncle Jimmy's, a church member who had seemed earnest and had given liberally to the church, stopped coming to church. He was warned that God would not bless his indifference, but he rapidly drifted spiritually and fell into several serious sins. Finally, to Jimmy's regret, he had to be dismissed from the church.

Bandit activity seemed to be more common than ever. Every night the missionaries heard shooting, and almost every night someone was kidnapped. Close by, a young girl and a married woman were taken. Then a few nights later two women were taken, one with a six-month-old baby. The robbers didn't care about the infant and threw it alongside the road. After a while they took the warm jacket from one of the women and released her. She eventually found the cast-off baby still alive, so she took it home. There was no word on the fate of the child's mother.

A town in which missionaries had established both a church and a school was overrun by bandits, looted, and then burned. The Chinese fire department came on the run, but their pomposity seemed to hinder their effectiveness. A man led the procession dressed in a yellow raincoat, blue tights, grass sandals and, on top, a brass helmet. Behind him were men lugging long poles with hooks and bright blue wooden tubs and buckets. Then came a wheeled cart with two pumps aboard and a clanging brass bell, drawn by men blowing whistles for all they were worth. The ladder brigade rounded a corner carrying one long bamboo ladder, and two men transported the hose in a big basket. A few stragglers with buckets brought up the rear.[1]

By the time the brigade got their act together, the fire had swept through the town, burning almost everything. Then, when it reached the house next to the chapel, the wind direction suddenly changed, and the chapel was spared. In fact, the Chinese Christians as a body were being largely spared from the kidnapping and killing of the roaming brigands. Only one had been captured during the past three years, and he had eventually escaped.

One night following an evening service at which Uncle Jimmy

had preached, pandemonium broke loose right outside the window. Assuming that he was the most conspicuous person in town at the time, Jimmy's first thought was that the bandits were looking to kidnap him. However, the bandits were attacking a home across the street, not 50 feet away. They kept up an incessant firing for about half an hour. Then he glimpsed a flicker of red and realized the house was on fire.

Later Jimmy learned that it was a particular man they were after. In the process they'd burned several homes to the ground, killed two men, carried one off for ransom, and slaughtered a number of cattle.

At about this time a Christian woman was kidnapped by robbers, and great prayer went up from the church for her release. Meanwhile, the Christians scraped together a large ransom for her release but delayed paying as long as they could. Just when they felt they must proceed with the payment, she suddenly appeared on the scene, free.

Apparently, the robbers had commanded one of their children to tie the woman's hands and lock the door to the room. The child did a rather shoddy job, and the woman finally managed to undo the ropes. Then she dug a hole through the dried mud wall of the house and escaped. Not a soul molested her on her rush to safety. After the shock of seeing her walk in the door, there followed great rejoicing. Many in that church recognized her escape as a modern counterpart to the story in Acts of Peter's escape from prison.

A woman named Mrs. Kao became a Christian. Despite her lack of education, she somehow managed to painstakingly read her way through two little books and was working on a third. When Aunt Sophie visited her after a time of absence, she found that, without prompting, Mrs. Kao had organized some church members into several small groups, and they were holding meetings in other villages. They led two services each Sunday in different locations, the services consisting of prayer, loud hymn singing, and preaching. Though some laughed at their biblical ignorance and lack of education, they were getting invitations from all around to "come and have worship" at various villages. Sophie wrote that if all Christians had their spirit, it would not be any trouble to get China evangelized.

Meanwhile, Mrs. Giang, the woman whose husband forbade her baptism, was still struggling. The husband had eventually allowed her to be baptized, but now he was demanding that she recant her belief in Jesus as Son of God. He shouted that if she refused, he would disown her.

She replied, "You can disown me and drive me away if you choose to, but I will never say or believe anything but that Jesus is the Son of God, for He is the Son of God."

Of course, the husband beat her at that point and claimed he'd have nothing else to do with her. However, what he really wanted was for her relatives to come around and plead for her so he could keep her without losing face.

The summer of 1922 was like that of most years. Summers were so searing that, typically, the Chinese in this region spent much of their time sitting around in thin attire, fanning themselves and sipping lukewarm tea. Along with the unbearable heat, insects and vermin were in their glory, so the missionaries did little traveling. They finished up odd jobs, did things they didn't have time to do during the rest of the year, and spent some time in the cool mountains of Kuling.

The fall freeze was a shocking contrast to summer's furnace. In the Grahams' home, though small tin stoves stood in almost every downstairs room, they failed to turn out much heat. They helped so little upstairs that the bedrooms were almost unbearably frigid.

"You would all go into hysterics if you could see how we are bundled up," Sophie said. "The rain freezes as soon as it falls, so I know it is cold, and besides, the howling wind does not help matters. So we have added clothing until I feel like an animated rag doll. I can hardly get my hands to my head, with ten strata of clothing between me and the outside world. My shoes are wadded with cotton and eiderdown, a pad of silk batting, and two pair of stockings. We get along very well, unless we're caught out in the open plains by these dreadful winds."

Uncle Jimmy was holding evangelistic campaigns throughout the region. With a group of six or seven, he went to each outstation. The church leader in charge of each station made all arrangements for meetings to be held in the churches and schools. The team stayed about a week in each station, working in the town on market days and out in the countryside on alternate days.

Jimmy described a typical day of evangelism. After an early breakfast the team engaged in an hour or two of prayer and Bible study. Then a team member would preach for half an hour or so on one angle of the Gospel story. After a break another would preach on a different angle and so on until lunchtime. After an hour or so for eating and rest, they would begin the same process again until it was nearly dark. Audiences changed throughout the day, but there was never a shortage of people wanting to listen. Some would stand for an hour or two, listening closely. After supper the Gospel team would gather for Bible study, discussion of issues and problems that had arisen, and prayer. He estimated that several thousand people heard the Gospel during the campaign.

Prayer was a prime focus during any meetings of this type. Jimmy observed that the faith of Chinese believers tended to be strong. They prayed simply and plainly, as to one with whom they were truly face-to-face. They always expected an answer, and usually received one. During the campaign a Chinese party from a distant city came to see Jimmy. Besides wanting to hear the preaching, they came to report that one of their church members was in dire straits with city officials. When he interjected that he didn't feel he could interfere with the authorities in the matter, the men answered that they didn't want him to intercede at all but only to pray to Almighty God with them regarding the matter.

Uncle Jimmy's next letter was dated January 4, 1923, and was labeled only "somewhere in China." The canal had frozen and stranded him on a little houseboat, leaving him, for once, plenty of time to write. He'd been assigned to oversee Dr. William Junkin's field while the missionary was home on furlough. So for several months he visited a total of 25 outstations and Christian schools in the district—doing pastoral work, examining inquirers, disciplining church members, and baptizing others.

In one city, Uncle Jimmy visited a penitentiary where regular services were held. When he went on Sunday to lead a service, he was met in the most cordial way by inmates who handed him a cup of tea and ushered him to a large group of orderly and attentive prisoners. Looking at their polite smiling manner, one would never suspect that they wore heavy chains on their ankles.

One of the prisoners with a life sentence had become a believer. That morning Jimmy spoke on John 3:16, and as he explained the love of God, he happened to glance at this inmate and noticed tears spilling from his eyes. But instead of reflecting misery, his face gleamed with joy.

There were others Uncle Jimmy met whom he described as "miracles of grace." One church leader had once been known for sheer wickedness. He was not only a bandit but a chief of bandits. Opium smoking, drinking, and gambling were among the least of his faults. He claimed with shame that there was little evil he didn't do, even resorting to torture and murder. Jimmy said it was difficult to imagine that this gentle giant was once a killer. The man had one of the kindest faces and softest voices he'd ever encountered. He was upright and was a great influence for good, always passing on the knowledge of God to those around him.

From mid-1923 until August 1924, the Grahams were on

furlough in the United States. One recurring reminder of the everyday stress of life in China was that Sophie, in the U.S., would sometimes wake with a start, involuntarily rising and listening for sounds of bandits. Then she'd realize where she was and drop back on her pillow with a contented sense of safety.

Jimmy and Sophie Graham on furlough,
in a photo taken in Charleston, S.C.

JIMMY AND SOPHIE'S GRANDCHILDREN
STANDING (LEFT TO RIGHT): JIMMY GRAHAM IV, MARY ABBOTT
SEATED: SOPHIE, TUCKER (ON LAP), MRS. LOUISE GRAHAM,
REV. JAMES R. GRAHAM III, LOUISE

SPEAKING OF THE UNSETTLED CONDITION
OF THE WORLD AT LARGE,
A WELL-KNOWN CHINESE GENTLEMAN
WHO HIMSELF WAS NOT A PROFESSING CHRISTIAN SAID
THAT IN HIS MIND THERE WAS
"NOT ONE GLEAM OF HOPE,
EXCEPT TO ONE CLASS OF PEOPLE,
THE BELIEVERS IN JESUS CHRIST,
WHO IS THEIR LEADER AND ON WHOM THEY RELY."

HE THEN NOTED A PUZZLEMENT:
"THERE IS ONE THING I CANNOT UNDERSTAND
AND THAT IS WHY THEY DO NOT SPEAK OF
THIS HOPE MORE."

CHAPTER 7

FAMINE

On their journey back to China, outside Shanghai the Grahams encountered, in their own words, "a little war, as usual." The warlords of Jiangsu and Chekiang were apparently peeved with each other and seemed to want to drag the surrounding regions into their jealous squabble. Cannon fire could be heard clearly along the rail lines, and all traffic had stopped. Even after so many years in the culture, Jimmy and Sophie never quite got used to how the Chinese people responded to some things in the world around them. In this case people were rushing around, carrying on business as usual while civil war raged all around them. They did not even seem overly disturbed at the many wounded or dead soldiers being transported into the town.

All the soldiers from Jiangsu Province had gone to battle, leaving not even a semblance of opposition to the bandits. But then government officials from both sides of the conflict took council with the bandits and bribed approximately 3,000 of them to participate in the war on one side or the other. What the Grahams feared was that, when the war was over, the bandits, now armed to the teeth with war-issue weapons, would return even more ferocious than before.

As the couple traveled to each of the mission outstations, they found many families who had lost loved ones by fire, sword, or rifle. One entire family was burned to death in their own home. What made it worse was the taunting and derision Christians had to endure for keeping the faith in spite of tragedy.

While in the field, the Grahams received word that fighters were returning from battle and had taken possession of their property. Upon a hurried return they found that it was soldiers, not bandits, who had moved in. The soldiers refused to budge, so an area church elder gave the couple temporary lodging.

It is to Aunt Sophie's credit that she was able to greet these events without yanking out her hair. She raved about a wonderful Christmas box received from friends in the States, and she hinted shyly how appreciated flower and vegetable seeds would be. "Most of us save a little spot of ground," she wrote, "in which we can squeeze some flower or vegetable. I just throw this out as a suggestion."

As a new year dawned, problems continued as additional idle soldiers returned to the area. About 150 soldiers appropriated a mission school and two chapels as a boarding house, and Uncle Jimmy could get no redress from the village council or the Chinese authorities. Also, in the Grahams' absence, outsiders had appropriated other church properties, and much tedious time was devoted to procuring other property.

However, Uncle Jimmy wrote home, "In spite of the difficulties, the autumn work has been most enjoyable, and please don't think that these drawbacks have in the least discouraged us. … 'Obstacles' is the middle name of missionary work and one sort of gets used to them."

March of 1925 marked the 35th year of the Grahams' service in China. Uncle Jimmy painted a picture of China that was vastly contrasting. At present, he reported, China was in a most pitiable condition. Hoodlums were everywhere, and soldiers were spreading over the country like grasshoppers—looting, robbing, and burning.

Conditions were worse than he had ever known them, and he compared the corruption to that of the old Roman empire. In contrast, he said that they had never seen the people give such interest and assent to the Gospel and that thousands had heard the message during the past few months.

One morning Sophie had a houseful of women who'd come to study the Bible. Suddenly the wind began to blow, and soon the heavens darkened with murky, whirling clouds of dust. The women continued to listen as if there were no storm at all, so she grabbed a feather duster in one hand, and whenever the dust covered a page, she'd whisk it clean. A thick coat of dust settled on everything. The women would slice a piece of bread and cover it immediately, but even so, their teeth ground on sand when they ate it. Still, valiantly, the women stayed on to hear more teaching.

God was working on every side. One Chinese preacher, who doted on his only son, almost lost the boy. Several thieves decided to kidnap the child for ransom. They walked into the house one night and woke the grandfather, demanding the child's whereabouts.

"The boy has gone with his mother to Mrs. Graham's Bible study class," the sly old man said.

The robbers believed him and didn't search for the child. Suddenly they seemed to panic and fled, leaving their guns behind. The boy they sought was only feet away, lying behind a thin matting.

A few days later the Grahams decided to send a barrow-full of furniture out to the country. They also gave the barrow-man $35.00 to deposit for them, a substantial sum in that place and time. The man was held up by robbers, but when they demanded his money, he replied that he was just a penniless employee. They searched his clothing and the barrow—every place but the right one. The man had placed the Grahams' package of cash in a dirty old hemp bag underneath the wheelbarrow. Throughout the day Sophie had prayed several times that the courier wouldn't be robbed, and she marked this as a clear answer to prayer.

Beginning with the end of May, in parts of China there was a great student uprising against foreigners, old treaties, and other things they thought important. In many Chinese government schools there developed a sort of mob rule, with students largely in the driver's seat. Sophie seemed to have studied the situation carefully, and she described it from her vantage point. She saw Bolshevism as a breeder of the trouble, which in turn lit fires of anti-foreign sentiment and self-serving pride and greed. It was primarily the students and the riffraff who entered wholeheartedly into the melee; it was not the "cream of China's people." And as a whole, the Chinese Christians refused to be roped into the conflict. Some even made the strongest sort of protest in the papers. Providentially, none of the mission schools fell victim to student rebellion.

Apparently there was also much controversy at this time in regard to America's policy of extraterritoriality for her citizens residing in China. The Grahams' view was that the protection of U.S. citizens in China was necessary in a dangerous, sprawling nation in which even many of China's own people were not protected from wholesale kidnapping, torture, and even butchering. Shanghai was under an extraterritorial treaty, and not only Americans but thousands of Chinese from the Grahams' region of North Jiangsu fled to Shanghai in violent times for peace and protection.

Sophie emphasized that she and Jimmy were not trusting U.S. protection in place of God's. She pointed out that they would not consistently go into robbers' dens with the Gospel if they didn't trust God wholly. However, she wrote, "I do believe God wants us to act reasonably and sensibly. I pray, 'Give us this day our daily bread,' and fully recognize that the food supply is in God's hands, but I should not feel justified in sitting still with my mouth hanging open when God has prepared means for us to use."

During the summer of 1925 the mission hospital expanded with a large, modern addition for women. They'd been turning patients away nearly every day, so this was a very welcome development for Drs. Bell and Woods. However, in October tragedy struck at the mission compound. The Bells' infant son, Nelson, Jr., developed amoebic dysentery at only 10 months. For 18 days he valiantly fought the illness, but finally his little heart could not stand the strain of the chronic high fever. Perhaps if he had been older, his system might have been able to overcome, but the little body quickly dehydrated and, in the end, nothing his skilled father did seemed to help.

He was buried in the brick-walled foreign cemetery in Tsingkiangpu where little Georgia Graham and many other American children had been placed before him. At the graveside Ruth Bell, her parents, and Rosa sang "Praise God From Whom All Blessings Flow."

Regarding the grief, Dr. Bell said, "Jacob limped the next morning after wrestling with God but that limp was because God had touched him. We may have a terrible sorrow which gives us an emotional limp, but it is where God in His love and mercy has touched us." [1]

Ruth and Rosa had grown into precocious youngsters, but there was a serious side to these children even during their earliest years. In view of the precarious nature of life in China, perhaps it is small wonder that, as a child, little Ruth's dream was to go as a spinster missionary to Tibet or be martyred in a far-off Chinese village for the sake of Christ.[2]

But there were also fun times for the children. Occasionally Jimmy and Sophie's grandchildren would come to Tsingkiangpu for a visit. Mary Abbott, the eldest grandchild, looked forward to exciting sleepovers with Ruth, whose mother would produce the most treasured pink and white marshmallows for them to eat. To this day, she still has a weakness for marshmallows.

As the political situation in southern China became increasingly unstable, warlords in northern China fought for dominance. Complex alliances resulted in two opposing armies, 60,000 strong.

Northern generals under Chang Tso-ling fought eastern and central generals under Wu Pei-fu. The armies collided at Tsingkiangpu, on November 1, 1925. The fighting raged so close to the mission compound that missionaries could hear bullets whining over their heads and see them spitting up dust. Neither side was fully trusted by the missionaries. According to Jimmy, soldiers in China "are an uncertain quantity, often more dangerous to their friends than their enemies."

For about five days heavy shelling continued around the North Gate area of the city. About 40 Chinese who were in the most imminent danger were offered shelter in Jimmy and Sophie's cellar. The terror of some was pitiable, but it became obvious that the Chinese Christians reacted with significantly less fear and panic than did the nonbelievers.

Finally, unable to take the city, a baffled General Chang withdrew north, leaving hundreds of dead soldiers as well as peasants who'd been caught in the crossfire. The fighting inadvertently provided an opportunity for evangelism as 400 wounded refugees passed through the hospital, and chapel services were held every day.

The constant struggle for power among warlords sometimes placed the missionaries in uniquely hazardous situations. One afternoon a passing warlord demanded that a particular city surrender to him. Having heard of this warlord's brutal streak, the magistrate knew his end may be very near, so he sent desperately for Dr. Junkin, a beloved missionary living in the Sutsien area. After some deliberation, Junkin offered to go in the magistrate's place and try to appease the warlord.

That night the huge city gates closed behind Junkin, and he walked alone across the prairie to face the waiting army. He was received very roughly but was finally able to get them to agree not to shell the city if he would guarantee a certain amount of guns, food, clothing, and other goods as well as the magistrate himself. The catch was that all this plunder must be brought in 20 minutes. When the city couldn't deliver in time, a frightful shelling began. Close to 1,500 terrified villagers piled onto Junkin's property and into his home as shells burst around them.

At last a party of wheelbarrows filled with goods pushed out toward the waiting warlord. Dr. Junkin went with them and begged on his knees for over an hour for the life of the magistrate. Throughout the night Junkin made five trips to the warlord's army in an attempt to save the city and lives within. Finally the magistrate and about 10 wealthy men of the city were kidnapped, but the city was saved. However, 10 days later, the magistrate and other kidnappees were returned unharmed. God had used a brave missionary to avert mass slaughter. A great thanksgiving service was held in the Junkins' courtyard.[3]

The belated annual conference for the Presbyterian missionaries was held that year at the Tsingkiangpu Mission Station. Eighty-seven adults and 50 children were present on the grounds, and Jack Vinson, one of the field's most loved and respected missionaries, served as gracious housekeeper to them all.

Uncle Jimmy then called in all the regional Chinese preachers for a 10-day conference of prayer and Bible study. He taught the Epistle to the Romans, and Sophie taught them a special study each day. She was a real favorite of the preachers, and Jimmy stated that he was always sure they were receiving good teaching from her.

Simultaneously with these meetings, Mr. Wang, a young evangelist, was holding services in the schools and the area church. As a student at the National Naval Academy, Wang had met a Christian young lady, and they'd married. Wang's wife began explaining the Bible to him. He was immediately interested and accepted it wholeheartedly as truth. After graduation from the Academy, he only served in the military for a short time. He felt compelled to begin preaching the Gospel. Though his home was in

Foochow, he spent many months each year holding evangelistic services in various places. He came from a wealthy family but did not depend upon that means of income. Still, his needs were always supplied. Uncle Jimmy was very impressed with his common sense and poise, his prayer life, and his command of Scripture.

Chinese churches in the region were struggling. Uncle Jimmy wrote home:

> My whole field has been so cut up by bandits, soldiers, battles, and general unrest that the work is getting very much disorganized. Church members have scattered and some have dropped away. The conditions in many places are not unlike what they had in Virginia and Georgia and other southern points during the American Civil War, with the added course of bandits; it is a wonder to me that the people have not become more demoralized. … At times like this it seems to me that life for them can hardly be worth living. But they do live on, in spite of the unspeakable troubles, and it's a constant inspiration to me. As I say, it is sad on one side of the picture, seeing this kind of thing all the time, but there is a joy to be gotten out of it that I wouldn't miss for anything.

Sophie spent several whirlwind months in almost constant Bible teaching. First, she traveled to Kiangyin, where she stayed with her niece, Nellie Sprunt Little, who had come with her husband as a missionary to China. Sophie taught a group of over 200 in Kiangyin for two weeks. Then she did a round of itinerating to the outstations with Uncle Jimmy. Back home again, she began teaching two Bible classes and preaching to women at two of the city gates.

Then some women traveled in from the countryside, and she taught them for three hours each day. One thing that impressed her was the spirit of faith evident among the women. They wrote down the names of those they wished to pray into the kingdom. Then they prayed both solemnly and impressively for two or three families at each meeting. One woman would say, "O Lord Jesus, save ——" (an individual by name), and all the others would call out, "Amen!"

Jimmy and Sophie both wrote home about an automobile that had been shipped to them by a woman in Florence, South Carolina. Sophie jokingly referred to it as the "Lizziemobile."

Jimmy claimed he was basically in favor of the auto, and Sophie stated assuredly that Uncle Jimmy was learning to drive it. Jimmy admitted, however, that friends in the mission station didn't think he knew enough to risk "his valuable life or his wife's, trying to drive it about the countryside."

It wouldn't have been too hard to learn if it were not for the unexpected stunts one had to master. The Chinese streets were so narrow that just turning a corner was frustrating. At most corners were vast arrays of pottery, reeds, baking goods, fresh meat, dangling garlic cloves, portable tea shops, and gambling wheels. Along straightaways one had to sit on the horn in an attempt to scare away wandering toddlers, sleeping dogs, herds of pigs, and men pushing loaded wheelbarrows. Meanwhile, a thousand-and-one kids would attach themselves to the spare tire and back bumper. Children also had the idea that dashing in front of an automobile would kill the evil spirits following them. Of course, the closer the car came to them, the more evil spirits were killed. Suicides were also common, and some Chinese could think of no better way to accomplish this than to step in front of a car. Girl babies were not nearly as desirable as boys, so tossing female infants in front of cars was not unheard of either.[4]

Jimmy thought the toughest thing was learning to "ford the streams, which are too deep even with a Ford." Sophie described their attempts to pass through causeways not quite as wide as the car, and their adventures ferrying the car across rivers. The most nerve-jangling feat was driving onto a ferry boat with barely three-inch margins on each side and making an almost right-angle turn in the middle of a canal from one boat to another!

In this same letter Uncle Jimmy made the only allusion on record of disharmony with Sophie, and he even related it humorously. They were in a room in a little mud hut, where one couldn't even yawn without the other person knowing what he was up to. She glanced at the letter Jimmy was writing to the churches in the States and said, "Whew! That's too long!" Jimmy said her reaction was both hasty and wrong, but he immediately admitted, "I usually mind her, as all good husbands do, so that letter died an untimely death."

During his itinerating circuit in 1926, Uncle Jimmy and Chinese church leaders examined about 500 men and women for church membership but baptized only 35. They also suspended seven from communion and dismissed two from church membership. He said they'd decided to require more spiritual understanding and maturity among inquirers before baptism and membership in order to ensure long-term faithfulness.

Though baptismal numbers were down, the Spirit of God was moving in the region. At one place near Tsingkiangpu approximately 100 families made the decision to give up idolatry. And Sophie told of five new believers who'd walked seven miles to be taught the Scriptures. The women showed up at her door soaked to the skin by a driving rain. She took them in, dried their clothing, gave them some dinner, sang with them, taught them "a whole lot," and sent them the seven miles home rejoicing.

In June one of Jimmy and Sophie's grandchildren contracted a type of typhoid and was sick for over three weeks. They rushed to the child's side, and when the child had gained back enough strength to travel, they accompanied family members to Kuling for a period of much-needed rest.

Kuling lay high above a Yangtze River gorge. This beautiful, secluded spot provided the missionaries with a place for refreshment and regrouping in an age when missionaries had to serve prolonged periods between furloughs and mission life could be incredibly stressful and demanding.[5] Mary Graham Reid, Jimmy and Sophie's granddaughter, recalls exhausting climbs with her father up the great mountain to Kuling, one section of which was called the "thousand-step" challenge.

These special times with family reminded Mary of visits to see her grandparents. She sometimes slept in the same room with grandfather. He always rose early, had his personal devotions, and did a rigid set of exercises. Then a Chinese hired helper would lug a tin tub into the bedroom and fill it with water.

With endearing modesty, Jimmy would tell Mary, "Now turn your head away while I take my bath."

Following the bath they would make their way downstairs to breakfast.

A missionary later wrote of his perception of Uncle Jimmy during these visits to Kuling. "Your love for God, loyalty to His Word, interest in the spiritual life of missionary and Chinese, and your friendliness toward friend and foe—how precious all those memories are to me."

When the couple returned to Tsingkiangpu, they found much of the region under famine conditions. In past famines the Grahams had some emergency funds which they could disperse in the form of staple foods, but this time there was no money available. Sophie wrote home, "If any of you feel inclined to give expression to God of your thankfulness that you are not a starving Chinaman or a worker among these awful scenes by a contribution, just send it to me and I will see that it goes to the distressed and worthy individuals."

Ever resourceful, she conceived a use for a small building in her front yard area. She had it repaired, fixed up nicely as a chapel, and then spread the news that every Friday, from dinner on, there would always be someone in the chapel to greet visitors and teach them about God. Many seemed glad to hear of it, and about 40 individuals showed up on the first Friday.

Sophie quoted a well-known Chinese gentleman who himself was not a professing Christian. Speaking of the unsettled condition of the world at large, he said that in his mind there was "not one gleam of hope, except to one class of people, the believers in Jesus Christ, who is their leader and on whom they rely.

"Now He is to return and will overturn and adjust affairs, and set all things right. In this is their hope so that they alone have any light before them."

He then noted a puzzlement: "There is one thing I cannot understand and that is why they do not speak of this hope more. I should think it would be the great subject of their preaching."

"Didn't this man," Sophie wrote, "give all of us teachers and preachers a proper and wise rebuke?"

Famine from drought was maddeningly replaced by famine from flood. The July-August rains were especially heavy and extended through September. Rains in the mountainous regions north of Tsingkiangpu were also torrential, resulting in rushing streams which poured into the Grand Canal, breaking through its banks and causing mass flooding. Many of the late summer and early fall crops, upon which the people primarily depended, were destroyed.

The Grahams' work among the outstations was paralyzed. In an appeal for united prayer, Uncle Jimmy wrote, "Some groups I have not visited at all—could not possibly get to them without wading in water waist or chest deep for miles. I have done this for a half-mile or a mile but it is hard to keep it up for too long a distance. Swimming is a fine sport and a useful one, but when you have to appear at the other end clothed and dry, it gets a bit difficult."

THE MISSIONARIES AT TSINGKIANGPU, JUNE 1931

STANDING (LEFT TO RIGHT):
REV. RUSSELL WOODS, MRS. A.A. TALBOT, MISS JESS HALL,
MRS. L. NELSON BELL (VIRGINIA), DR. L. NELSON BELL,
MISS LUCY FLETCHER, MISS ELINOR MYERS, ROSA BELL,
MISS CASSIE LEE OLIVER (WEARING WHITE CAP), MISS MARY MCCOWN,
MRS. JAMES B. WOODS, REV. A.A. TALBOT, DR. JAMES B. WOODS.

SEATED IN CHAIRS:
REV. AND MRS. JAMES R. GRAHAM II (UNCLE JIMMY AND AUNT SOPHIE)

ON GRASS (LEFT TO RIGHT):
HAM TALBOT, BILL TALBOT, VIRGINIA BELL, TOMMY HARNSBARGER,
RUTH BELL (HOLDING PRINZ)

EVEN IF HE WANTS US
TO SUFFER MARTYRDOM
FOR HIM,
WE SHOULD BE GLAD
AND SHOUT FOR JOY,
FOR GREAT IS THE REWARD
AWAITING SUCH IN HEAVEN.

—SOPHIE GRAHAM

THE BLOOD OF THE MARTYRS
IS THE SEED OF THE CHURCH.

—TERTULLIAN OF CARTHAGE, CIRCA 200 A.D.

CHAPTER 8

MARTYRS

Christmas without family in 1926 loomed as a lonely time until the Grahams received an invitation from the Bells to join them for breakfast and a family celebration. A few minutes before the appointed time, a messenger knocked at the Bells' gate bearing gifts from Uncle Jimmy for each child. Each gift was a dried ox tongue with a name card affixed on a hook. Even though ox tongues were a coveted delicacy among the Chinese, the American children were dismayed. However, soon Uncle Jimmy arrived, spilling hilarity into the house and caught up in delight at the prank he'd pulled. Many decades later the Bell children still recall that Christmas with laughter.

The Bells had a mountain of presents sent from many friends and relations, and Sophie said she and Uncle Jimmy enjoyed the opening of presents almost as if they were theirs. After a delicious breakfast, everyone hurried to the mantelpiece to retrieve their Christmas stockings, which were filled with oranges, candies, nuts, cough drops, tubes of toothpaste, etc.

The Chinese had prepared a special Christmas service amid colorful festoons and paper lanterns, bells, and balls. The little Chinese fellow who preached used grandiose hand gestures and such animation that it would have been amusing if it hadn't been so good and appropriate. Following the meeting, everyone returned to the Bell home. In the light of the gorgeous Christmas tree in the Bells' garret, 12 children stood with their heads thrown back, singing carols for all they were worth. Then, as at other times, Uncle Jimmy read aloud a Tugboat Annie story from one of Nelson Bell's old issues of the *Saturday Evening Post.* He frequently had to stop reading because of his convulsive laughter. It was a day that lifted the spirits of both families.

The political scene in China during this period was stormy as usual. In many areas anarchy reigned. Anti-foreign and anti-Christian sentiment was snowballing, and the U.S. seemed to be doing little to protect her citizens in China. Uncle Jimmy sounded quite alarmed and, for the first time, Aunt Sophie wrote, "One just wonders if our work here is finished."

Though she expressed deep faith in God, she did not minimize the peril: "I cannot imagine anything more desperate than existing in this country without the assurance of God's presence and protecting care. Even if He wants us to suffer martyrdom for Him, we should be glad and shout for joy, for great is the reward awaiting such in Heaven."

The crisis in China had not developed overnight. The popularity of a leader named Chiang Kai-shek was on the rise. He had succeeded Sun Yat-sen, who died of cancer in 1925. Chiang outmaneuvered the ambitious Mao Tse-tung, and for a time many Communists joined forces with him, hoping to use his Nationalist Party as means to a Soviet-style revolution. Though not a Communist (nor yet a Christian), Chiang Kai-shek, for his part, hoped to use the Communists for his own purposes. He launched his famous "Northern Expedition"—all the way from Guangzhou to Shanghai. This triumph unified southern China and, most vitally, gave the Nationalists control of the lower Yangtze.

Their success against the Peking regime in southern China inspired Chiang's forces, and by July 1926, they drove into northern China, gaining control of the upper Yangtze valley. Nanking fell in March of 1927, and many foreigners, including missionaries, were killed. Then Shanghai fell. It seemed only a matter of time before northern Jiangsu Province was attacked.

Anticipating possible emergency evacuation, for months Sophie had not gone to bed at night without laying out her clothes and shoes so that she could jump right into them if the need arose. At the end of March the American consulate ordered missionaries to leave China. The couple repeatedly sent telegram warnings to their son, James III, and his family in Yencheng to evacuate, but they received no response. Finally they hired a special messenger to deliver a rushed message.

Other missionaries on the compound evacuated, but Uncle Jimmy and Aunt Sophie remained—one day, three days, six days—then a message arrived that their son had fled by sea. Early the next morning Jimmy and Sophie took a boat on the first leg of a journey toward Haizhou, meeting up with the Bells and others who had left earlier. The journey north across the Yellow Sea to Tsingtao was thankfully uneventful except for the inclusion of 3,000 Chinese refugees, who packed the boat almost to overflowing. Then followed five days of great suspense, as the Grahams waited for news of their son. Finally he arrived with his little family on a Chinese junk to a reception of great rejoicing.

The Grahams and several other missionaries decided to head for Shanghai, where thousands of British and French troops as well as American Marines now protected the city. Discouraging news of military looting and destruction of missionary homes and schools filtered back to them. However, Chinese Christians were doing well, holding regular church services, and the mission hospital was functioning on a limited basis.

The Bells sailed on to the U.S. and stayed there until 1928 when conditions improved somewhat and China opened again. In the meantime soldiers had occupied their home and destroyed the hospital equipment. But providentially, they did not find most of the Bells' belongings, which were sealed in the attic.

Uncle Jimmy's take on the Nationalist victors was not positive. Though their propaganda machine avowed sympathies which sounded quite benign, in practice he viewed the so-called Nationalists as rabidly anti-foreign and often anti-Christian. He did not, in fact, see them as significantly different from the long procession of militarists who had marched across the stage since 1911.

Some Christians in the U.S. were bewailing the fact that "the work and toil of all these years has been ruined in a few terrible months." But Jimmy and Sophie viewed this idea as not only dishonoring to God but patently untrue. Throughout this trial, though often disappointed and hurt, the couple consistently maintained a trusting attitude.

"All the talk of Christianity being a failure in China, and the church being wiped out," said Jimmy, "is just so much bosh. I am as sure of a wonderful future for [the Chinese] as I ever was."

Sophie added, "As to the Chinese, many will seem to fall away and discourage many, for this is the chaff blowing away. But the many, many true will never fall away, even if it means the loss of this life. Discouraged? No! Faith shaken? Oh no! A tighter grasp on Him while He calls us to walk in the dark by faith and not by sight? Yes, by all means, yes."

The Grahams spent a number of months in Shanghai, and Jimmy carried on some administrative duties for the churches in North Jiangsu through use of the mails and three or four intermediaries. Some Chinese friends had been kidnapped, some murdered, and church members' property burned, but few actual church members had been kidnapped, and the Christians were as involved in the church work as they'd ever been. Thankfully, very few of the Chinese believers had forsaken the church or denied the faith.

By early February 1928, much of the fighting in the Tsingkiangpu region had ended, and Uncle Jimmy and a missionary associate returned to the area. When they first arrived, they found the countryside as bandit-ridden as ever. But some soldiers led by a military-trained individual succeeded in surrounding one large body of bandits and practically wiping them out. The bandit population went into hiding, and there was a respite from violence. But when the soldiers moved on to other areas, the bandits soon became active again.

Jimmy was extremely busy trying to visit all the churches in his area, which now covered approximately 1,000 square miles. He was greatly encouraged to find about 250 adults ready for baptism. Some churches had suffered from lack of organization, but it was gratifying to find that the great mass of church members had held fast. Generally speaking, there had not been a severe persecution of Christians. However, some individual incidents were horrifying. One Catholic priest over 70 years of age was dragged behind a horse for miles and then finished off with exquisite tortures.

When Sophie joined Uncle Jimmy in October, she threw out a challenge to prayer supporters: "Do you remember how you once prayed the bandits out of the country? By the time we were ready to make our rounds to the churches there was not one bandit around because all had been mobilized to fight in the army. Three times, God in a marvelous way has cleared the track for us in answer to prayer. So I am giving you a grand work to do which takes thought and hard work but no money."

The Grahams' home in Tsingkiangpu was not evacuated by soldiers until December. Their belongings had been stripped, straw was strewn all over the floors, and filth was everywhere. The locks on all 40 doors in the house had been smashed, and cigarette smoking and small army stoves had blackened the ceilings and walls.

First, all the refuse had to be removed, and the ceilings had to be scraped and whitewashed. Then sulphur was burned, and the walls and floors were scrubbed down with water and soda. The clean floors were then rubbed with kerosene oil and finally painted.

Sophie spoke of "one of the sweet things in connection with the calamity." Friends permanently leaving China decided to give all of their household goods to the Grahams, and this took much of the sting out of the great loss.

In January of 1929, Uncle Jimmy had to travel to Shanghai for 10 days of committee meetings. This brought a tartly comical reaction from Sophie: "I am opposed to the number of committee meetings and am fully convinced it is a smart way the Evil One has devised to take people from work they could not otherwise be persuaded to give up."

Sophie herself began a Bible study that overflowed out of her parlor and hall into the chapel outside of her home. She also attended several funerals of individuals whom she had led to salvation.

One was an elderly lady who turned to Christ from Mohammed. Shortly before her death she said, "How fortunate, how fortunate I am that Mrs. Graham and her helper came and told me about Jesus, my middle-man and Savior. And I am not going to hell, but I am going to heaven with Him."

Another was a young lady whom Sophie had known since the girl's childhood. She'd been converted from a pagan home and had become a fine witness for Christ. After a long illness, one day her breathing became very labored, and Sophie came to the bedside and sang softly to her. While she sang one hymn, the tortured expression on the girl's face became a peaceful smile, and she sang with Sophie,

"There is rest in heaven for the weary one; there is rest for me."

As she died, Sophie rejoiced that God had allowed her to lead the young lady to Christ. "All the years out here are nothing," she said, "in comparison with one soul saved to eternal life."

Sophie heard about a young man named Calvin Chao who had contracted tuberculosis and was extremely ill. As a former student in the school James Graham III administrated, Calvin, named after the great reformer, had distinguished himself both spiritually and academically. There was no one available to nurse Calvin back to health, so Sophie volunteered. While continuing with her regular duties, somehow she fed and treated the young man, teaching him further in the Scriptures.

Calvin gradually recovered and after some months reluctantly left the Grahams' home. It wasn't long, however, before he was back in Tsingkiangpu introducing Uncle Jimmy and "Mother Graham" to his new Christian wife, Faith. The couple eventually had eight children, one of whom they also named Calvin.

Calvin Sr. became an evangelist and moved to the U.S. There he founded a small Chinese seminary in Los Angeles. He and Faith also carried on a good ministry of hospitality in southern California for many years, inviting Chinese into their home, sharing the Gospel with them, and teaching them.

While the Grahams were traveling, the soldiery had absconded with both the Grahams' car and their motorbikes. They'd also conscripted the area wheelbarrows and barrow-men to serve the military, so Jimmy and Sophie had to begin traveling long distances by rickshaw, which was more comfortable than wheelbarrows but also much more expensive. Jimmy, however, was grateful for the rickshaws for Sophie's sake, as she was "getting on in years." As for him, he claimed he didn't feel much older than he had 30 years before, except after a grueling week or two of travel to outstations.

James III had recently returned to China and was dedicating

himself primarily to itinerant evangelism. He received an invitation to conduct a series of meetings some distance up the Grand Canal, but he got a late start. When he reached the canal, the boat had already departed.

This was no small problem. Boats upriver were not of easy access, and villagers in Jiangsu Province had traveled far and wide publicizing the meetings and planning to accommodate the crowds. What a waste and what a disappointment! James sat down on a rock and cried out to God, "Lord, what an unfaithful servant I am. How can you forgive your messenger?"

Guilty and discouraged, James stood and began walking slowly down the road. As he trudged along, he noticed a large compound nearby. Circling it, he came to a gate, which he entered. Soon he realized it was a Buddhist monastery. There were steps leading up into the temple and on the steps sat a Buddhist monk, his head bent between his knees. James sat down beside him and began speaking. Since James spoke Chinese like a native, the man assumed this was a common villager and mumbled replies without looking up.

Finally he asked the monk, "Why are you here?"

The man replied, "To repair my soul," and began describing the severe fasting and other deprivations he was practicing.

James said, "Have you ever heard of the Father of the Heavens?"

"Oh yes, I have."

"Did you know that He has a Son who came to earth to repair the souls of humanity? Mere humans could never do that; the Lord Yiesu came to pay the price for our sins and that pleased the Father of the Heavens."

Suddenly the Buddhist's head popped up, and he gazed into the face of this foreigner for the first time. His eyes were wide and wondering.

"Did this Father of the Heavens send you to tell me about His Son, Yiesu?"

"Yes, He did."

That day the monk turned from darkness to light. Soon he left the monastery and, like the woman at the well, went into the nearby town and told everyone he saw about this Son of the Father of the Heavens. A church was formed in that place, and James returned many times through the years to preach there.

When the time rolled around for the annual missionary conference, Jimmy was ill with fever and could not travel by rickshaw, so the couple hired what Sophie termed a "tin lizzie." When it arrived for them, Sophie claimed it looked and sounded as if it consisted of car parts picked out of a trash heap and strung together with wires. When asked if they really thought the heap would reach the destination, the operators acted very surprised and insulted and assured them the vehicle was in perfect working order. Sure enough, with much jiggling and bumping they arrived in good time at the mission meetings.

That summer it was Sophie's turn to become ill. On a warm night near the end of June, she went to sleep with her window open. During the night a chilled east wind sprang up, and by morning she was shaking with cold, a terrific pain shooting down her spine. The diagnosis was erysipelas, caused by the streptococcus bacteria. She went into a coma and lingered very close to death. Dr. Bell sent out a flurry of telegrams, asking for fervent prayer on her behalf. Everyone in the hospital, from doctors to servants, devoted themselves to prayer. Chinese women poured in from all directions, inquiring about their beloved Aunt Sophie, and even many men traveled in from the country to show their concern.

Finally, after a full 16 hours, Sophie regained consciousness. Five weeks later she was still resting and gaining back her strength, anxious to get back to her evangelistic work.

By the close of 1929, Uncle Jimmy and his new associate,

Addison Talbot, had examined about 1,500 inquirers, and 300 were baptized into church membership. Uncle Jimmy had also been busy reopening quite a number of the country mission schools. The Nationalists had announced a law forbidding Bible teaching or any religious teaching in schools, but the missionaries decided that they would continue teaching the Bible and see whether the law would actually be enforced. If enforced, the missionaries planned to shut down all schools, as they were unwilling to lead Bible-free schools.

In the spring, evangelistic services were held throughout Uncle Jimmy's region. Most of the preaching was now done by Chinese pastors. On weekdays they traveled to neighboring areas, preaching outdoors on market days and in surrounding villages on alternate days. Then on Saturdays and Sundays, they were back in their own pulpits. The churches had grown to a point in which much of Jimmy's time was now spent on administrative duties. He expressed obvious delight at the growth but regretted at times that he was no longer doing as much direct preaching and evangelizing.

It was of real concern to him that, with all the responsibility involved with regional church outposts, he simply had no time to concentrate on church-planting in his home base city of Tsingkiangpu. He did marvel, though, at what Dr. Bell and his staff were able to accomplish, both physically and evangelistically, among the people there. How Bell was able to evangelize, practice medicine, devote time to family, and fulfill unexpected demands without burning out, he did not know.

Sophie's recovery from her near-death experience was agonizingly slow. Because she had to give up most of her itinerating, she concentrated what little energies she had upon evangelism in Tsingkiangpu. Once, following a Sunday service in the city, a woman came up and said, "Mrs. Graham, you must come over to my home and I will invite all the women I know to come and hear."

In ways like this, the Gospel continued to spread. Sophie did attempt one ministry trip to the country. Her health demanded that the journey be made in an automobile. She would teach a session and then go to bed and rest, regain a bit of strength, and go back to teaching again.

Occasionally Uncle Jimmy would walk over to the mission hospital and ask for a little brandy. Once, when one of the medical personnel asked him why, he said that at times Sophie was so exhausted that she couldn't even teach her ladies' Bible study. If she took a few tablespoons of the brandy, it revived her enough that she was able to go and teach for an hour or two.[1]

There is an amusing story about Aunt Sophie and brandy. Being a dyed-in-the-wool Virginian of the old school, every Christmas she simply had to have traditional fruitcake. So she gave the recipe to her Chinese cook, and he assembled the ingredients and chopped up the nuts and fruit. Then, in an attempt to behave beyond reproach, she took the bowl of ingredients into her pantry, closed the door, and privately added the brandy. Then she dutifully gave the bowl back to the cook to bake. The following Christmas, the cook prepared the ingredients and went to find Sophie. "Mrs. Graham," he said, "it is time to go in the pantry and add your brandy."

Most farms in the communities Jimmy and Sophie frequented were so small that two or three plantings had to be done each year. This was often done like clockwork. Jimmy said that one morning he passed a field of wheat waving in the breeze. That evening he passed the same plot, and it had already been reaped, ploughed under, and planted with sweet potatoes.

He described a common sight around the farms which was, to him, a poignant reminder of the biblical Book of Ruth. When any field was being harvested, poor people would line the field with rakes poised. The moment the harvest was completed, they would rush onto the field, desperately raking up any stray kernels of grain left behind. For some, such scavenging was their only means of survival.

"The field has also been producing other kinds of fruit," reported Jimmy, "spiritual fruit. I have never known a greater willingness among the people to listen to the Gospel." He had recently examined approximately 1,600 inquirers and baptized 152 adults.

In August Sophie had another bout with erysipelas, but fortunately it was a relatively light case, and after eleven days of complete rest, she felt significantly better. In fact, she seemed to minimize the dangers of disease in contrast to the threat of kidnapping or murder: "The fact is," she wrote to prayer supporters in the U.S., "your missionaries have no idea what may happen at any minute. We may finish our days and never be kidnapped; on the other hand, we may be taken tomorrow and with cruel hands be tortured or killed.

"Now that sounds gruesome," she continued, "but not more so than the fact that any of your motorcar riders there may, tomorrow, have a few broken bones, be minus a leg or two, or actually be dead. We are all in God's hands and our trust is in Him anywhere and at all times."

Her warning of cruelty was not exaggerated. A town in which the Grahams had established a promising church was attacked that very month. The robbers burned half the town, pillaged it, and slaughtered about 200 people.

Bandits also raided the town of Yang Jia Ji. When missionary Jack Vinson traveled there to check on the welfare of the converts, the marauders captured him as well as a number of Chinese.

A government force pursued the bandits, and the kidnappers offered Vinson his freedom if he could persuade the force to withdraw. He said that, if they freed him, they must also free the other prisoners. When the bandits refused, Vinson elected to remain with his fellow prisoners.

Still weak from a recent appendectomy, Vinson could not keep up with the fleeing group, and one of the bandits began menacingly jabbing him with the barrel of a gun, acting as if he may shoot.

"If you shoot me," said Vinson, "I'll go straight to heaven."

When they reached a stream with muddy banks that made it difficult to cross, Vinson fell on his face in exhaustion. The head bandit called back to his men to leave him there, but instead they shot him and brutally beheaded him. Before the ordeal was over, 35 Chinese hostages would also lie dead.

In a great demonstration of courage, missionary Ed Currie walked right into the bandits' lair and brought back Jack Vinson's body to Haizhou for burial.

As news of more killings drifted in, Sophie rushed for comfort to Proverbs 3:25–26: "Be not afraid of sudden fear, neither of the desolation of the wicked, when it cometh. For the LORD shall be thy confidence, and shall keep thy foot from being taken" (KJV).

At times tragedy followed upon tragedy. Ed and Gay Currie served at a mission station about 100 miles north of Tsingkiangpu. Nelson Bell had run the mission hospital there in 1920 while the resident doctor was on furlough. During that period, the Bells and Curries became close friends.

On the morning of November 24, 1930, a housekeeper left the Curries' three-year-old son, John Randolph, unattended for several minutes. He fell headlong into a caldron of boiling water. Moments later the child died in his mother's arms. What made this death even more devastating was that only a few years earlier their three-year-old daughter, Lucy, died of botulism after wandering into a pantry and eating contaminated string beans. In their grief the Curries could only cling to God and trust a mercy they could not fathom.[2]

But there was also good news of the Holy Spirit's power in the land. A rumor had been making the rounds that a number of officers and soldiers from Chiang Kai-shek's Nationalist army had become Christians. The rumor was put to the test when a horde of 50,000 soldiers under the command of a General Chang Chi Kiang passed through cities along the Grand Canal in the early fall of 1930. As James Graham III stated, most Chinese armies passing through left an area "like Sheridan left the Valley of Virginia." However, this force paid for what they got and made no trouble of any kind. They behaved like true Christians.

General Kiang then toured the province of North Jiangsu, studying living conditions and deciding how they might be improved. As he went from place to place, he preached so courageously and frankly of his faith that people began calling him the "flaming evangelist." Christians were impressed to see such a devoted believer among those in military authority. So zealous was Kiang that some said General Chiang Kai-shek's Christian baptism had been primarily due to Kiang's witness and instruction in the Scriptures.

Jimmy and Sophie spent much of the winter and early spring of 1930–31 traveling. Their teeth needed attention, but they'd declined going to native-trained dentists. In an effort to show their skill, these dentists would display all the teeth they'd extracted on a long string—some of the "better" dentists had 1,000 to 1,500 teeth on display. They did do a beautiful job carving interesting scenes on gold teeth they installed, but the forceps and other tools they used looked scary—certainly less efficient than those seen in an average auto mechanic's shop.[3]

So between itinerating trips to church outposts, Jimmy and Sophie went to Shanghai for dental work and, while there, spent some time with their daughter Sophie who had just been assigned to a new post in Suchowfu. Then with her they went to the fall Presbytery at Sutsien, reuniting there with James III and his family and staying on to celebrate Christmas together.

In February James III and his wife also needed extensive dental work, so Sophie offered to care for the children in their absence. Two days later one of the children came down with the measles, and in a few days all four were quite sick. Sophie nursed them night and day for several weeks until their parents returned. So, though the days were not all pleasant, the grandparents were pleased to spend some all-too-rare time with family during the winter.

A spring filled with church work warmed into another sweltering summer that slowed everyone down to a feeble crawl. On June 26, 1931, Jimmy and Sophie were scheduled to board the S.S. President Wilson to the United States for furlough. Considering that Sophie's health was still significantly limiting her activities, the following comment in a letter to friends is amusing: "I do hope nothing will happen to delay us, for it is evident to me that Mr. Graham is in need of the change and rest. These last few years have been a severe strain on him."

Initially the Grahams had planned and carefully saved the money to return to the United States by way of Europe. They were excited about touring several countries on the continent. However, shortly before their departure the Grahams reported that they had decided not to visit Europe. The truth was that they'd given the extra money to the poor. When questioned, Aunt Sophie only said, "I'm not crazy about Europe anyway. One of these days, when Christ comes, I will have a resurrected body. Then I can go to Europe anytime I want to."

It is also remarkable that, in spite of the inevitable missionary desire that a furlough be partly a period for rest and rejuvenation, Jimmy spent one two-year furlough attending a medical school and another one attending a business school—all with the motivation of serving the Chinese people and the mission more fully and expertly.

While on this furlough, the Grahams missed another of the natural catastrophes for which northern China was known. Mass flooding broke through the banks of the Grand Canal at Sutsien. By early August two ancient bridges in Tsingkiangpu were underwater, and the new foreign-built bridge was being threatened. Some missionaries took a boat down the canal, bound for Shanghai. Four hours after they passed one city, a typhoon swirled through, and the bank broke in 13 places. If the missionaries had been there, they would surely have drowned.

That December Uncle Jimmy wrote to church supporters from Virginia, grateful for the restful months and for the opportunity to reunite with old friends and family in North and South Carolina, Virginia, West Virginia, and New York.

Of China he stated, "It looks as if the Lord has had a controversy with China and our hearts bleed for the old land. It looks as if He were doing drastic surgical work on it and its people to cure their soul's disease. All of these great troubles in the last 50 years have been followed by some level of spiritual awakening, and I have no doubt that will be the result of these trials overwhelming the land now. I have never known in my life a greater willingness to hear the Gospel and I believe this is quite generally true through all the field served by our North Jiangsu Mission."

RUTH BELL AT TSINGKIANGPU
WITH HER EVER-PRESENT COMPANION, PRINZ.

CALVIN AND FAITH CHAO AND THEIR FAMILY.
AFTER AUNT SOPHIE NURSED CALVIN BACK TO HEALTH FROM TUBERCULOSIS,
HE BECAME AN EVANGELIST AND THEN STARTED A SEMINARY.

JIMMY AND SOPHIE'S DAUGHTER SOPHIE JR.
ALSO SERVED AS A MISSIONARY IN CHINA.
HERE SHE IS SHOWN (CENTER) WITH MEMBERS OF
ONE OF THE CHURCHES WHERE SHE TAUGHT BIBLE CLASSES.

THE DISTRICT IS FAMINE-STRICKEN
AND BANDIT-RIDDEN,
AND THE PEOPLE HAVE SUFFERED MUCH
FROM RECENT WAR.
BUT IT SEEMS THAT ALL
THESE AFFLICTIONS HAVE HAD A VERY FAVORABLE
[IMPACT] ON THE ATTITUDE
OF THE PEOPLE TOWARDS THE GOSPEL.
THEY WELCOME US AS NEVER BEFORE
AND THROUGH THE WONDERFUL POWER OF GOD
MANY HAVE FOUND THE WAY OF SALVATION
IN THE LORD JESUS.

CHAPTER 9

BAPTIZED!

B_y the end of September 1932, when most of the flooding had ebbed, the Grahams were back in Jiangsu. Those at the station gave them a homecoming welcome. It was the warmest of reunions for a group that treated one another as family in the best sense of the word.

Jimmy testified, "The times of stress and strain, of famine and sickness and danger seem to have bound us together with cords of steel and I am glad of all the experiences for their beautiful results."

Jimmy's niece, Fanny Graham Taylor, and her husband had enjoyed that beautiful unity as they served on the Tsingkiangpu mission compound for 10 years. In 1927, however, they were torn from their missionary family and transferred about 100 miles south where the dialect was different and they had no friends. At times, the loneliness was excruciating.

Due to the Depression in the U.S., the couple's salary was cut. Also for financial reasons, when they were due for their first furlough in seven years, the mission board delayed it for another year. At 3:00 a.m. on a frost-encrusted October morning in 1931,

Fanny crept out into the yard and cut her own throat.[1] She was buried in a cemetery overlooking the Yangtze River, where the great J. Hudson Taylor and his wife also rested. Furious at the Mission Board for their apparent insensitivity, Dr. Bell wrote a blistering letter of rebuke.

Missionaries took two more heavy hits in 1932 from a couple of unexpected sources. First, a commission of American laymen under the chairmanship of Harvard philosopher William Hocking determined to assess the state of American missions overseas. The group was made up primarily of theologically liberal modernists.

As a result of their study, the group released a report entitled *Rethinking Missions.* It was a heavy-handed report which criticized the accomplishments of medical missions, deplored evangelism, and claimed that missions should be primarily humanitarian since "man is not eternally lost because he knows not Christ."[2]

The missionaries at Tsingkiangpu were offended. Dr. Bell wrote, "It is our constant aim to help the bodies of these people all we can, using all the skill we possess and also trying to keep up with latest developments in medicine and surgery, but we still believe the soul of the patient is infinitely precious, and it is our constant prayer that God will help us do the best job we can on their bodies, that through this we may point them to Christ who saved us and who is so willing to save them."

The commission also claimed that "the use of medical or other professional service as a direct means of making converts or public services in wards and dispensaries from which patients cannot escape, is subtly coercive and improper."

Calling the findings an "ill-odored" report, Uncle Jimmy said of hospital evangelism, "I will say that we do not take the patients by the throat to compel them to listen, nor do we lock them in; there are a couple of doors to each chapel and a large courtyard outside where anyone wishing to can go. They can also come and go whenever they feel so inclined."

The second broadside blow came from Pearl Buck, daughter to Absalom Sydenstricker, the co-founder of the Tsingkiangpu mission station. She had written a book entitled *The Good Earth,* which won the 1931 Pulitzer Prize. Not realizing that she sympathized with the religious liberals, the Southern Presbyterian Mission sought to honor her at the Waldorf-Astoria in New York. In her speech on that occasion, Buck called for an end of preaching and urged that the Spirit of Christ be manifested only by one's lifestyle. She caricatured evangelical missionaries as ignorant, arrogant, superstitious, and crude. The speech was published in the *Literary Digest* as "Is There a Place for Foreign Missions?"

The missionaries at Tsingkiangpu responded to the speech with outrage:

"It is unthinkable that one should go as a missionary and have in one's heart the knowledge of God, His Son our Savior, and the offer which He makes of eternal life to all who believe and then remain silent. Nor can we imagine greater conceit than to imagine that one, simply by one's own force of personality and attractiveness, could win one soul to Christ."[3]

The Grahams were now close to 70 years of age and mission leaders urged them to curtail their exhausting field work and concentrate on ministries in Tsingkiangpu. Jimmy said giving up the country work was like "losing an eye tooth" but he grudgingly agreed to the wisdom of it. Sophie spoke wistfully of "missing my dear country people," and she relished their occasional visits to her in the city.

Jimmy worked mostly among the hospital patients, speaking in the chapels and visiting in the wards. As churches at the outstations had grown through the years and developed native leadership, Jimmy's work had evolved more into training leaders, administrating, and organizing. So he was gratified to be again sharing the Gospel with individuals on a daily basis.

Sophie stayed busy teaching Bible classes nearly every day, visiting extensively, and entertaining many in her own home. She loved hospital evangelism too but stated, "I admit I am a bit too sympathetic, for I find myself tossing back and forth all night thinking of and praying for the poor sufferers I've been with."

Sons and daughters of the missionaries often faced the momentous decision of whether to stay in the U.S. after completing their education or return to their roots by serving in China. The contrasting pull could at times start early. Once a visitor to Tsingkiangpu asked several of the missionary children what they wanted to be when they grew up. One said a missionary; one said a fireman; one said a nurse. William, a son of Dr. and Mrs. James Woods, thought awhile before answering, "I want to be a missionary on furlough."

Despite the allurements of America, the young man who eventually took over the Grahams' circuit to mission outstations was Russell Woods, William's brother. His parents had served right there in Tsingkiangpu for decades. Uncle Jimmy marveled at the inherent advantages the sons and daughters of missionaries enjoyed when they returned to their home fields. They usually had a solid familiarity with the language from the start, and they knew the people in their disposition, culture, customs, and point of view in a way, Jimmy reported, "that we other and older poor mortals only get after many hard knocks and mistakes."

The Southern Presbyterian Mission in China had seen an unusual number of her sons and daughters return as missionaries. In fact, of the 26 families who had been at work there since 1889, 22 now had representatives back in China or in other mission fields, altogether totaling 39 individuals. When Jimmy wrote of this in 1933, six or eight additional young adults were trying to return but could not because of lack of adequate funds.

In spite of the Grahams' own limited funds it is remarkable how generous they were. Uncle Jimmy loved to send Christmas or birthday gifts to missionary kids being schooled in the U.S.

Rosa Bell acknowledged such in a letter written from Wheaton: "This is to say thank you for my Christmas gifts and to tell you that I love you. I think that I'm going to use the $5.00 in getting a Chinese water pipe. ... And the stationery just hit the spot and I know my school friends will be tickled pink to have letters from me written on it."

The Grahams' financial ledger is very revealing. During one brief period, these are only a few of the expenditures:

Help old woman-	.20
Hunan famine-	5.00
Helping blind man-	1.80
Help build church near Sunming-	2.00
Assist Yang Kiadswang church-	20.00
Rumanian traveler-	3.00
Help Pole and Russian-	2.00
Helped wounded soldier-	1.00
Help two Russians-	1.00
Relief Crippled Soldier Fund-	5.00
Assist flood sufferers-	10.00

Keeping in mind that salaries were dramatically smaller then than now, it is difficult to ascertain how the Grahams retained enough money to keep body and soul together.

Along with thousands of medical successes, there were heartbreaks for Dr. Bell. Hsi Si-fu had been head carpenter for the mission hospital for many years. He was courteous and dependable, but every attempt to share the Gospel with him had been rebuffed.

One day he casually told Dr. Bell that a dog had bitten his hand as he was returning from lunch. When Bell asked if the dog was rabid, Hsi said no, it was just a neighbor's dog. He had flipped his hand at it, and it snapped.

"I wonder if we hadn't better give you the anti-rabies treatments," said Bell.

"No, doctor. That dog's not mad, I know it."

Two weeks later Bell came down the steps of his home and found Hsi at the foot of the stairs.

"Doctor!" he said hoarsely. "I can't swallow. I can't swallow."

At that moment Bell knew Hsi Si-fu would die within 24 hours. Tests bore out the grim truth, and the doctor told Hsi gently that his death was imminent. Family and friends rushed to the man's side.

When Dr. Bell had a chance to be alone with him, he said, "Hsi, you have rabies and you know you will die. All these years you have heard the Gospel, yet you have never accepted Christ as your Savior."

As he explained the Gospel again, suddenly Hsi understood. He knelt at his bed, confessed his sin, and professed faith in Jesus as Savior. Then he told his son and his wife that they must have Christ too.

"Do not burn incense and paper money," he said, "or carry out any heathen practices when I die."

This was the greatest proof of his conversion because these rituals were deeply ingrained in the Chinese mind. Hsi asked to be transported home by rickshaw, for he wanted to die there. Between bouts of pain and choking, he told the gathered neighbors that he now believed in Christ and they must do the same. At 7:00 a.m. the next morning he died. In a letter during this period, Dr. Bell told the recipient that he felt such grief that he still couldn't speak of the experience.[4]

At about this time, Drs. Bell and Woods learned of a cure for a disease of the spleen called *kala azar*, which was unusually common among the Chinese. It was caused by a parasite in the blood which dangerously enlarged the spleen. The mission hospital commandeered buildings nearby and were able to house about 150 of these patients at any given time. Approximately another 400–500 kala azar sufferers stayed in other area housing for the 40-day treatment.

The prolonged treatment period offered an excellent opportunity to communicate the message of Scripture to any patients who were interested. Besides this, there were some Bibles, gospels, and excellent Scripture tracts on hand which patients could take back to their villages when they were released from the hospital.

As a method of follow-up, contact slips were given to patients to bring to Christian leaders in their area, and the leaders were sent a duplicate slip. In that way, many of the ex-patients found a church and continued under Christian influence.

Uncle Jimmy reveled in his direct witness to hospital patients. To U.S. churches he wrote, "It is a lovely job and I often wonder why the whole lot of you do not storm the Committee rooms demanding to be sent out to take a part in it. Of course, you could not all come, but you would have the satisfaction of having tried."

The Depression in the U.S. continued to cause a serious shortfall in foreign mission funds. In an effort to give churches an accurate idea of the enormity of the North Jiangsu field and the funds needed, Uncle Jimmy laid out the numbers: "The territory is approximately as large as Virginia and North Carolina combined and has about 14,000,000 people in it. There is probably no more densely populated area of equal size in the world. We have 83 regular missionaries, including wives. There are about 480 native full-time workers, partly paid by Chinese and partly paid by the Mission, and there are 260 places where services are held, 40 organized congregations, representing well over 8,000 individuals. There are now also about 75 schools with about 2,000 pupils."

Jimmy then made a fervent appeal:

In 1929, we received in American dollars, $68,000. This has been cut yearly until, for this year, 1933, we are promised only $12,000. During this period, the salaries of the missionaries has been cut four times for a total of 33 percent. The result of the above has been that helpers have been dropped, chapels given up, hundreds of schools closed, and several thousand pupils let go. Hospitals which last year treated about 200,000 patients, have been forced to go on a self-supporting basis, which means a vast decrease in the charity work offered. Our plans for aggressive work among the unevangelized has had to change drastically, for the heathen cannot be expected to support workers who wish to tell them something they naturally do not care to hear. It is heart-breaking to see so much of [the ministry], as it were, thrown on the scrap heap. I am writing to urge you to try and put the idea of the desperate condition over to your people.

In spite of the report of far-reaching growth of the Chinese church in North Jiangsu, some at home still doubted the sincerity of the people. Once, an old school friend of Jimmy's told him, "If you're honest with yourself, you know there are no sincere Chinese Christians; practically all of them are just 'rice' Christians—just entering the church for benefits they can gain from it."

Jimmy replied that most people who made remarks like that had never spent any time in the Chinese church. They also failed to understand that church discipline among the Chinese was often infinitely more strict than among American churches and that those counterfeits tagging along for alleged temporal benefits were cut from Chinese church rolls.

A related idea that had made the rounds was that only the poorest of the poor, the uneducated, and those of no social position became Christians, presumably for the supposed prestige it gave them. Jimmy admitted that even in Christ's ministry the poor and sorrowing usually accepted the Gospel more gladly than the wealthy. But with a little honest inquiry, a person would discover a number of wealthy, educated Chinese in the church.

Uncle Jimmy was happy to mention only a few in his region. He said, "Some of the most prominent members of the Chinese government are Christians and they don't care who knows it. The true dictator of China and both the outgoing and present Ministers of Finance, with their wives, are all church members."

He listed more in a letter to the States:

One zealous new Christian is a young man who has done post-graduate work and is on the committee for drafting a new constitution for China.

Of three young men I have recently baptized, one is a university professor, the second, manager of a large business, and the third, a university student planning to go into Christian work.

A Chinese couple who graduated from prestigious New England colleges were led astray spiritually by modernist professors, but are now devoted Christians advancing the gospel of Christ.

A young man with one of the brightest minds I have ever encountered in China also forsook Christ while a university student but after recovery from serious illness, has returned to the faith and now spends much of his time witnessing to others who have drifted from the faith.

Though bandit activity had ebbed somewhat by this time, it remained a palpable danger. In the fall of 1933, three bandits appeared at a door, asking if the man of the house was home. It was the home of Mr. Gao, one of the leading elders in the Chinese church. When told that Mr. Gao was not at home, they rushed into the house and kidnapped his two sleeping children, aged eight and one and a half.

This stirred up the Chinese Christians in the area unimaginably, and they gathered together for around-the-clock prayer in small groups. They were praying for four things, that the children would be returned, uninjured, without paid ransom, and that God would be glorified in everything that occurred.

One must understand the human impossibility of what the church was asking. Bandits were ruthless and would get their ransom, even if it required the sending of various severed body parts to the parents. So it was an undeniable miracle when, a week after the kidnapping, the Gao children were returned without injury and without a ransom.

Satan's work was not limited to violent or illegal activities outside the church. In a 1934 letter to the U.S., Uncle Jimmy described what surely had to be one of the strangest and most difficult days of his missionary experience.

One Sunday he was preaching to a congregation about the power of Satan and how he was the ultimate source of evil and sorrow in the world. One woman became increasingly restless and a fierce, angry expression appeared on her face. When he contrasted the power of Satan with the overcoming power of Christ, the woman exploded. During the next 15 minutes, there was pandemonium in the church as she hurled blasphemy and profanities. Many men and women in the congregation began to pray aloud for God to show His power and relieve the woman from this evil power. Her hateful shouting decreased until she was just moaning quietly.

Uncle Jimmy opened his eyes and saw one of Sophie's elderly "Bible women" stand and place her hand on the head of the lady. Her prayer was as tender and beautiful as anything he had ever heard. When she finished, the woman fell over in an exhausted faint. The people picked her up and laid her on a bench, and when Uncle Jimmy left a few hours later, she was still asleep from fatigue. In due time she was admitted to the church and rejoiced in her newly found joy and freedom from evil control.

On the very same day at a different location, he was again preaching about the powerful character of Christ and His victory over evil. As he preached, a woman in the group became increasingly restless. Suddenly, with a loud cry she began cursing and blaspheming Christ and calling on people not to believe on Him. She was wild and uncontrollable, obviously in great agony.

A church member intervened and announced that the woman was demon-possessed and that the family was begging the church to pray for her and cast out the devil. Uncle Jimmy asked the family if they wished him to pray and if they would promise to do away with idolatry to worship God alone. They assented, so the formal service was adjourned, and a fervent prayer meeting commenced, with many believers praying. Gradually the woman began quieting down and seemed to be lapsing into a coma-like state. Finally she lay on the ground unconscious but breathing quietly. The following Sunday, she was present with a happy, peaceful expression on her face, and she rarely missed a service after that.

However, Uncle Jimmy feared for the woman, especially during the Chinese New Year, during which there was much idol-worship and revelry. Following the holiday, he visited the same church again and sensed in the woman a troubled spirit. When he asked whether she'd practiced any idolatry, she admitted that she had and a that demon was again oppressing her. Jimmy warned her clearly and prayed with her for strength to resist anything that would forfeit God's presence and blessing. From that time on, there was no trouble and about a year later she was joyfully baptized.

At a communion service some time later, Uncle Jimmy recognized the woman's husband and son appearing for baptism. When asked why they wished to be baptized, they answered that it was because they had seen the power of God in transforming their wife and mother and they wanted that same presence in their own lives.

In his letter Jimmy mentioned that a number of demons had been cast out through the years and that God had truly "freed folks from the terrible incubus which was ruining their lives." Wisely, he admitted that some whom the Chinese thought were demon-possessed were not so, but were victims of various physical or mental illnesses. It required spiritual insight and experience to discern the differences between psychiatric problems and spiritual ones.

At about this time, in the region of Suancheng, Jimmy and Sophie's son, James III, was invited to preach some evangelistic messages. A new missionary couple named John and Betty Stam were in the area. Betty had grown up in China as the daughter of Presbyterian missionaries. Her parents, Charles and Clara Scott, still lived and served in Tsingtao. At age 18, in 1924, she had transcribed and adopted for herself the very same prayer that Uncle Jimmy considered his life-covenant prayer, the prayer ending with the words:

> **Use me as Thou wilt, send me where Thou wilt**
> **Work out Thy whole will in my life**
> **At any cost now and forever.**

It is possible she learned the prayer from Uncle Jimmy at some point in her youth. Now married and back in China, she and her husband enjoyed James Graham's messages. In fact, John appreciated them so much that, when he was invited to preach in Kinghsien, he asked James III if he could present the same messages. Shortly after, the Stams departed on a three-week evangelistic tour covering a circumference of about 200 miles. During this tour they passed through Miaosheo, the very city in which, not too long in the future, they would exemplify the full measure of that life-covenant prayer.

Sophie's ministry among the women in Tsingkiangpu continued to grow and flourish. She felt great sympathy for believers who were persecuted in their homes for the faith. Two young women in particular could only attend occasional Bible studies secretly. With tears on her cheeks, one told her, "I do believe in Jesus.

He knows I believe but I am not allowed to come and worship Him."

A female patient in the mission hospital was the wife of a city official in a city quite distant from Tsingkiangpu. She told Aunt Sophie how she made the decision to seek treatment. For eight months she had suffered, receiving no relief from Chinese doctors. Then, on several different nights she had a dream in which a man she had never seen before told her she must go to the hospital in Tsingkiangpu. Finally, accompanied by a servant, she traveled to the hospital. Within five days she was greatly improved physically, but more importantly, she was now an enthusiastic believer.

The woman hungrily consumed every hymn, every verse of Scripture, every Gospel tract given her. She said she planned to set up a little chapel in her hometown and gather 20 or more of her friends with whom to share the Gospel. Then, when they were trained, these would go out and preach to others. Sophie had rarely seen such a contagious Christian.

Her work was interrupted in March 1934, when James III asked her to travel to Chinkiang and care for their children for several weeks. Some time before, her daughter-in-law had contracted erysipelas and had not been able to gain back her strength, so Sophie made it possible for her to enjoy a protracted period of complete rest. She reported that she got along "finely with the five children" and the hired help.

Late in the same year, Dr. Ken Gieser and his wife, Kay, arrived at the mission station. Ken was to provide much-needed medical assistance to Drs. Bell and Woods. Of course, the first months were a time of radical adjustment for the Giesers. Learning the language was one of the greatest challenges. One morning at breakfast, when Ken warned the house boy that the stove was getting too hot, he was met with a cold glare. He learned later that, instead of saying *"lu tsi"* (stove), he had said *"k'u tsi,"* which meant he thought the boy's pants were getting too hot.[5]

Once, at a Chinese feast someone politely placed a cooked

duck's head into Kay's bowl. She almost fainted. She didn't want to offend the host, but she didn't want to gag on a duck's head either. With her chopsticks she hid the head under her place card, and the waiter finally had pity and carted it away.

Kay listed some of the other difficult adjustments:

Some think that individuals should have smallpox while still in childhood. A favorite stunt of grandmothers is to give it to the babies.

If children under eight years old die, they don't bury them. They generally wrap them in some matting and randomly leave them someplace.

They place a gold ring in the nose or ear of the small boys so the evil spirits will think the child is a girl and leave it alone.

Chinese point with their chins, not with a finger.

One doesn't accept a gift right away—hesitate and stall, stall and hesitate—and then accept.

Spitting on the church floor is very common, as is shelling and eating peanuts.[6]

The Giesers adapted to many of the Chinese foods, but pig's nerves turned out to be a bit much for their palates. Once at a men-only feast, Uncle Jimmy said to Ken, "Son, do you know what you're eating?"

When Ken shook his head, Jimmy said, "Snakes!"

It was sea-slug soup, and Ken actually liked the stuff.[7]

Even some of the mysterious Chinese food was more enjoyable and distinguishable than the British cooking at the mission home at Shanghai. Nelson Bell had a favorite joke about the mission home: "A man once went into the place for some refreshment. After tasting the chosen beverage, he told the waiter, 'Mister, if this is coffee, bring me cocoa. If this is cocoa, then bring me coffee.'"[8]

Kay Gieser began accompanying Sophie on hospital visitation three afternoons each week.

"Aunt Sophie is ever so dear with the folks," she said. "She listens to their troubles so patiently and sympathetically, then talks to them most simply and beautifully about Jesus. Some listen intelligently, some giggle nervously, some are indifferent, some are already believers … it's a wonderful opportunity to reach many."

Sophie would tell patients that Kay was the new doctor's wife and they'd make all sorts of personal comments about her body or clothing. One elderly woman even picked up Kay's skirt to see how far her stockings went and what she wore underneath her Chinese dress.[9]

Though the Grahams were no longer able to travel the circuit to the many mission outstations, in 1935 Jimmy was asked to assist in the country communion services and the examinations for baptism. The examinees in one church ranged from 12 to 84 years of age, and in social and financial status they ranged from beggars to directors of business firms, from farmers to engineers and professors. It was a true cross section of Chinese life.

Jimmy described the examination of an elderly lady who was 84 years old and quite deaf. In fact, her hearing was such that it was hopeless to ask her questions regarding the details of the Gospel. However, the session had observed her lifestyle, her constant church attendance, her prayers, and her desire for salvation. When she appeared before the session, one member stood and shouted at the top of his voice in her ear, "Old grandmother, do you believe and worship the only true God?" She said yes, violently nodding her head.

"Do you know you're a sinner?"

Another vigorous nodding.

"What will you do to be saved?"

"I pray to Jesus," she said emphatically, "and trust in Him."

The whole session almost broke out in a cheer of delight.

Without taking a vote, they shouted out, "Old grandmother, you will be baptized tomorrow."

She left the room, her face wreathed in a smile.

Tallies of growth on the entire North Jiangsu field in 1935 were mixed. There were 27 additional outstations established during the year, making a total of 301. And there were now 42 church bodies, 20 ordained Chinese pastors, and 204 Chinese church leaders (56 less than the previous year because of drastic cuts in mission contributions). Still, it was very gratifying to missionaries on this field that Chinese churches were becoming increasingly self-governed and self-supported.

Through the hospital ministry, 217,000 patients had received care in more ways than one. A Chinese female evangelist would later testify, "Time and again I have met people in the country who have put away their idols and who believe the gospel and who say they first heard it while a patient in this hospital."[10]

Total church membership in the region was about 10,000, plus approximately 13,000 individuals who had been examined for membership but had not yet received admission. The 129 Sunday schools nurtured approximately 7,400 pupils, and Chinese contributions for churches and schools totaled about $11,000. Of the offerings, Uncle Jimmy stated, "You might think that is not much, but you can have no conception of the dire poverty from which it came."

Jimmy acknowledged that all the lists and figures regarding the Chinese church were a "statistical blast," and he wondered if readers found them monotonous. "However," he added, "the facts given here can be pondered with profit and thanksgiving!"

UNCLE JIMMY AND AUNT SOPHIE IN THEIR GARDEN
IN LATER YEARS IN TSINGKIANGPU.

MISSIONARIES IN CHINESE DRESS, PREPARING TO FLEE
BY RAIL FROM THE JAPANESE IN 1940.

MISSIONARY FAMILIES EVACUATING AHEAD OF
THE JAPANESE ATTACKS BEGAN THEIR JOURNEY TOWARD
THE COAST ON A CANAL BOAT.

JAMES R. GRAHAM III (FARTHEST BACK) AND OTHER
MISSIONARIES PREPARING TO EVACUATE ACROSS OPEN WATER ON
A CHINESE SAIL SHIP.

THE COURAGEOUS CREW OF THE CHINESE JUNK THAT HELPED
JAMES III AND HIS GROUP ESCAPE.

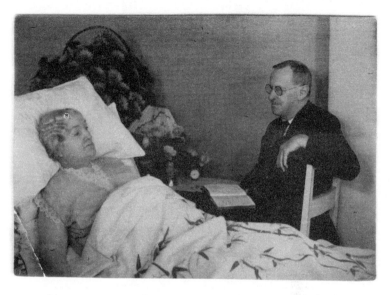

JIMMY ATTENDED SOPHIE IN THE HOSPITAL IN SHANGHAI
AFTER HER STROKE, FROM WHICH SHE DID NOT RECOVER.

DON'T THINK, I PRAY YOU,
THAT YOU ARE NOW USELESS IN YOUR OLD AGE.
THERE IS STILL ONE GREAT WORK THAT YOU CAN DO
AND THAT IS INTERCESSORY PRAYER.

—WU YUNG CHUEN,
CHINESE EVANGELIST

CHAPTER 10

LEGACY

On the Chinese political front, after Chiang Kai-shek's invasion of northern China, he turned on the Reds, intent on "eliminating the cancer of Communism." In 1934 he ordered the Nationalist army to assassinate party members and labor organizers. The Communists were forced to abandon their urban bases. As the Nationalists closed in on their prey, the Communists broke out and started running. Their journey lasted a full year and came to be known as the "Long March." They left Jiangxi province about 100,000-strong and headed west into Yunnan province in southwest China. Then they turned north, past Sichuan province, eventually ending up in Shaanxi with only 4,000–6,000 stragglers.[1]

Christians around the world were shocked and saddened in 1935 by an event that was widely reported in the international news media. Red soldiers on the Long March kidnapped missionaries John and Betty Stam. Realizing what was happening, Betty Stam tucked some paper money into her baby's clothing and hid the child, praying that some Chinese Christians would find her and save her life. The Communists led John and Betty up a hill outside

Miaosheo, 200 miles north of Tsingkiangpu, stripped them of their padded clothing, then forced the local population to come watch as they beheaded them.

Their child, Helen Priscilla, was discovered two days later after a Chinese pastor heard whispers from an old woman about where the infant might have been hidden. Chinese Christian mothers lovingly volunteered to nurse the hungry baby. With the money Betty had concealed, the pastor arranged to smuggle the child to safety and had her taken to Betty's parents, Charles and Clara Scott, in Tsingtao. [2, 3, 4]

As they often did, the Grahams spent the summer of 1935 in Kuling. Sophie's health was gradually declining, and with it, her physical energy. Her letters became less frequent. In a letter from Kuling on April 1, she wrote, "Please do not think you are out of mind because my letters are few. I am like an old clock that must be wound up often to keep running and sometimes stops! But my interest, love or prayers have not stopped …"

This letter was apparently her final one to churches at home.

In the awful heat of the summer, she sometimes found it difficult even to participate in daily activities. While in Kuling for the summer, she saved up all her strength for Sundays, when she would attend a large preaching service led by her son, James III, or other invited speakers such as Watchman Nee, Griffith Thomas, or Dr. Donald Grey Barnhouse.

Many of the educated upper class Chinese were attending such classes. As they became believers, they would often begin holding what became known as "parlor Bible studies." They invited a number of friends and relatives to their homes and asked a good Bible teacher or preacher to present the Gospel to them. The informal setting allowed for a relaxed atmosphere, and attenders felt free to ask any questions that came to mind.

James III was often asked to lead such studies, and the questions flew so hard and fast that he sometimes didn't leave a home until 10:00 or 10:30 at night.

In Kuling, wealthy Chinese women would also invite Sophie to tea, and their main topic of conversation was often about how to get their husbands and friends to hear and believe the Gospel.

Back in Tsingkiangpu some months later, Sophie suffered a stroke and became partially paralyzed. Uncle Jimmy began dividing his time between hospital evangelism and caring for her.

He described an interesting experience during this period. As he walked down a city street one morning, he heard what sounded like a parade coming in his direction. Then he saw a company of soldiers blowing horns, with cavalrymen coming along briskly behind. Bound securely by hands and feet with new rope, a condemned man was riding a rickshaw in the middle of the procession. A policeman walked beside him, holding a rope tied around the man's neck. The accused was sitting in a dazed lethargy, smoking a cigarette that had undoubtedly been given to him per his final request.

The man was intentionally being paraded down the principal streets of the city with a notice hanging above his head and telling his name and crime. Great crowds trailed the procession. Uncle Jimmy marveled that so many took pleasure in something he would have gone 10 miles out of his way to avoid.

As they drew closer to the place of execution, people surged forward in callous eagerness. They shouted and pointed fingers in the alleged criminal's face, laughing and cruelly deriding him. Uncle Jimmy viewed it as a sad exhibition of the natural bent of human nature. It struck him that this must be a very similar picture to what happened when the Lord Jesus was led through the streets of Jerusalem.

He said, "It has led me to understand better the sordidness of all He, the Ruler of the universe, went through of contempt and disdain for our sakes and for our sins, and it makes me appreciate His love for me more than ever."

One day, after a particularly difficult week, Ken Gieser was walking toward the Bell home, shoulders slumped.

Uncle Jimmy saw him and said, "Son, are you a bit discouraged?"

Ken nodded. "I can't seem to learn the language the way I should. I'm having a hard time getting hold of the administration of the hospital, and I find that there's so much to learn medically in preparation for Dr. Bell's leaving."

"But you should never give in to discouragement."

"That sounds rather theoretical to me at this point," Ken answered. "I don't see how a person can work in this land without being discouraged occasionally."

"When we first came to Tsingkiangpu more than four decades ago," said Jimmy, "Sophie and I rented a small home and I would go out to the country to preach and pass out gospels and tracts for two or three weeks at a time. Invariably I would come home with black and blue marks on my body after being chased from one village or another. Sophie would have a hot water bath for me and after a few days of recuperation I'd go out again. I did this month after month for 14 long years before people began coming to Christ. But I always figured that this was what God wanted me to do and the success of my efforts was entirely in His hands. There was no room for discouragement."

Uncle Jimmy paused and grinned. "Son, go to work. Never get discouraged. You are doing what God wants you to do. You're faithful to the task and that is all that matters."

Ken said that throughout his life this brief conversation stood as a powerful enduring lesson to him.[5]

Since the late 19th century the Chinese had been embittered by Japan's gradual expansion into Manchuria, the northeast region of China with three provinces and more than half a million square miles of farmland, forests, and mountains rich in coal, iron, and precious metals. The land had been promised to China for their supposed support of the Allies during World War I, but instead, it was deeded to Japan.

By the early thirties Japan's incursions were rapidly escalating. In March 1932, the Kwantung Army completed the occupation of Manchuria, creating the puppet state of Manchukuo, which became an industrial and military base for Japan's expansion into Asia. The Japanese policy of aggression would escalate and culminate a decade later in the bombing of Pearl Harbor, an attack that turned out to have a personal impact on one of Jimmy and Sophie's grandsons. But no one envisaged that event in the 1930s.

In July 1937, the Japanese attacked Chinese troops at the Marco Polo Bridge near Beijing, beginning the occupation of northern China. That same summer, Chinese Communists and Nationalists curtailed their own civil war and united against Japan in an attempt to end the violation of Chinese territory. Though it seems beyond imagination, by the time this war ended, 20 million Chinese would die of war-related injuries.

There was an immediate effect on one American girl. The month following the Marco Polo battle, Ruth Bell, now a mature teenager, was to leave China to continue her schooling at Wheaton College in Illinois. It was at Wheaton that she would meet and win the heart of a tall young man named Billy Graham (no relation to Jimmy or Sophie Graham). On the very day Ruth was to depart, the Chinese forces retaliated by attacking the garrisoned Japanese in Shanghai. The superior Japanese weaponry prevailed, and thousands of Chinese fled the region.

In view of the danger, Dr. Bell delayed his daughter's travel plans, and Ruth was elated. Despite the threat, she much preferred staying in China with her parents. Several days later, the Japanese actually attacked the Tsingkiangpu airfield, though the bombs did minimal damage. By September 1, the American ambassador was urging the missionaries at the Tsingkiangpu station to flee for the U.S.

The Grahams had been in China for 43 years and Sophie was now quite helpless. However, neither the Grahams nor the Bells wished to leave China. As the messages from the American consul rose in urgency, the missionaries asked vital questions: *How would the disabled Sophie be transported safely? How much baggage could be brought? Would they proceed directly to Shanghai?*

Finally on September 8, a voice over the radio told the "stubborn missionaries" that they were being warned for the final time. By the 17th, the Bells and Grahams began traveling north on the Grand Canal by launch, transferred to a houseboat to Suqian, and took a train to Haizhou, where the Japanese were shaking the city with some of the most severe bombing of the war. The Bells' daughter Virginia remembers all the passengers evacuating the train and lying in ditches during one bombing run. After the journey resumed, the train moved along an open stretch of valley. Japanese planes reappeared high in the sky, circling into attack formation. As the missionaries prayed, the cloud cover closed, and the attackers veered away to search for more visible targets.

Escaping Haizhou without injury, the missionaries were taken by a small Chinese boat to a prearranged rendezvous with an American destroyer, the USS Pope, waiting 10 miles offshore.

The Yellow Sea churned wildly, waves slapping waves. Each time the Chinese boat bumped momentarily against the destroyer's side, one person would make the treacherous leap across. But no one knew how to transfer the helpless Aunt Sophie. Everyone held their breath as Chinese boatmen prepared to try to lift her toward the outstretched arms of the American sailors. Knowing the great hazard, Uncle Jimmy prayed in an audible voice to God for peace. Almost immediately the water seemed to calm; the Chinese boat slipped softly alongside the destroyer, and Sophie was gently handed off to the waiting American arms. The instant she was firmly on deck, the wind whipped up again and frothy waves flew high. Ruth and Virginia Bell witnessed the miracle. Years later, Ruth said that, whenever events of life encouraged her to question God's omnipotence, she remembered that prayer in the middle of the Yellow Sea.

The destroyer had traveled less than a mile when nine Japanese warships, external lights extinguished, appeared through the mist. The vessels circled the destroyer, then unexplainably went slowly on their way. Finally, at 1:30 a.m. on September 19, the Bells and the Grahams were set ashore in Quindao (Tsingtao), 110 miles from Shanghai.

They were not in the least intimidated or fearful. Uncle Jimmy wrote to U.S. churches, "We are in port somewhere—quite a few are gathered here in Tsingtao. … But we are sitting, figuratively, on the front doorstep, planning to go back at the very first opportunity. The object of this letter is not to tell you of trouble in China; we have lived next door to trouble ever since we came to China. There has never been a time in my forty-eight years of life here when there was more of a call to hear the gospel and a greater willingness to listen to it."

At a time when most would be seeking encouragement from others, Jimmy offered some: "There is no reason for you to feel discouraged. Nothing in what is now taking place should dampen your ardor or cause you to cease in your prayers for this work or to decrease by a penny whatever money you are now contributing."

While in Tsingtao, the Bells stayed with Charles and Clara Scott, Betty Stam's parents. Mrs. Scott especially enjoyed having Ruth Bell around because she thought Ruth reminded her of Betty. Before Ruth departed for the U.S., Mrs. Scott gave her books and articles about Betty's life and martyrdom as well as some of Betty's poetry.

Although the rest of the Bell family returned with other missionaries to the Tsingkiangpu station a few months later, it became evident that it would be too taxing to attempt moving Sophie there. After some weeks in Tsingtao, Jimmy managed to have her transported to Shanghai, where they were forced to "retire." A rough tally indicated that, during the years in itinerant evangelism,

Jimmy had traveled by wheelbarrow the equivalent of the planet's circumference at least three times and many more miles by cart or rickshaw. Jimmy was certainly not inactive in his new home either. He made it his business to gain an awareness of the diverse Christian work being accomplished in this bustling region of over three million people.

Meanwhile, Nelson and Virginia Bell missed mightily the presence of Jimmy and Sophie at the mission station. Bell even wrote the Presbyterian Mission headquarters in the U.S. asking whether they could be escorted back to Tsingkiangpu and allowed to live in a residence on the mission compound. Mission director Darby Fulton demurred: "Looked at purely from the standpoint of general policy," he wrote, "I feel sure the Committee would not regard this as wise. When a missionary is retired it's expected that his direct connection with the missionary organization on the field should cease. Of course, some missionaries might remain on for several years, occupying mission property and helping with the work ... but others would create diverse complications and difficulties. As a uniform policy, I am sure that experience would prove that the wisest thing is for the missionary to seek residence and work elsewhere."

At about this time disturbing word reached Dr. Bell of Presbyterian intentions for the North Jiangsu Mission. At a time when Dr. Bell and those at his compound felt an overwhelming need for more workers, Mission authorities were considering opening a new mission in a west China region which would employ North Jiangsu missionaries waiting in Shanghai and those detained temporarily in the U.S. To Bell, this was "the last straw."

Bell reiterated the great need North Jiangsu missionaries were experiencing for some assistance and relief:

"What about the McLaughlins, alone in Haizhou for seven months already, carrying an almost intolerable burden? What about the four missionaries at Suchowfu who have passed through unspeakable strain doing a work which has commanded the attention of even the public press? Is there to be no relief for them? What about the four in Huaian who have been bombed and their homes partially wrecked while co-workers were killed almost before their eyes? What about Marguerite Mizell, carrying on for months the load of an entire station?"

Bell closed his letter with a touch of self-deprecating humor: "All I have written which is beside the mark, just charge up to the present strain and a naturally argumentative disposition."

Shanghaied in Shanghai, Uncle Jimmy attended many of the denominational and independent Christian churches flourishing in the city. Throughout 1938 and '39, the church had been conducting what they called a "Crusade for Christianity," which was similar to what Westerners would call evangelistic meetings. Thousands had accepted Christ as a result of these services.

In Hangchow, six or eight Christian colleges and about 15 high schools had combined into a union. Jimmy was quite impressed with the comprehensive, organized way students were taught the Scriptures and integrated into local churches.

As a result of the war, Shanghai had seen a massive influx of refugees—at least several hundred thousand strong. Very effective means were also being used to reach that group with the Gospel. Of this work Jimmy said, "While the destruction wrought here [in northern China] has been enormous and the results most pitiful to look at, yet in God's providence, it has resulted in many, many people who would probably never have come in contact with the Gospel, hearing about it and accepting it."

In a letter to Uncle Jimmy, a Chinese evangelist named Wu Yung Chuen seconded his conviction. He wrote, "The district is famine-stricken and bandit-ridden, and the people have suffered much from the recent war. But it seems that all these afflictions have had a very favorable [impact] on the attitude of the people towards the gospel. They welcomed us as never before and through the wonderful power of God many have found their way of salvation in the Lord Jesus."

Chuen went on to entreat Uncle Jimmy for prayer: "Don't think, I pray you, that you are now useless in your old age. There is still one great work that you can do and that is intercessory prayer. Pray for God's work and pray for me, too, that when I come to my old age I may, like Paul, say, 'I have fought a good fight; I have finished my course.'"

Missionary W.H. Hudson also needed fervent prayer. He wrote Jimmy from Kashing Christian Hospital in Chekiang, China: "Our property here was badly damaged during hostilities. ... Our churches were burned, wrecked, occupied, or looted; but now, after two years, reorganized and going on much as before. Evacuation may mean more loss and dispersion of the church, but the invisible church in the hearts and souls of the converts is indestructible."

During two awful weeks in the winter of 1937-38, Nanjing was attacked by Japanese forces, and when the dust cleared, 300,000 Chinese lay dead of atrocities in an infamous episode that became known as the "Rape of Nanjing." Back at the mission station the Bells and several other missionaries continued their work as heavy fighting moved steadily closer. In August 1938, a battle termed "Bloody Saturday" took place between Chinese and Japanese forces in the Shanghai region, but there was still relative peace in Tsingkiangpu.

Nelson Bell wrote a prayer letter to the U.S. which reflected a dread of the possible conquest of their area because of the "destruction of life and property and the unbridled lust, rape, murder, and looting" he knew would result. Meanwhile, he was experiencing some of his busiest days in the hospital. He described one such day in the same letter:

A little before five in the morning, saw a woman who

needed an immediate Caesarian section with hysterectomy. This was successfully carried out before breakfast but I missed hospital prayers. Issued drugs to pharmacy. ... Made rounds in women's surgical wards. Then the following operations: amputation of breast for cancer, removal of stone in bladder, operation on chronic mastoid, incision of large carbuncle of the neck. Got through in time for last few minutes of staff prayer meeting. Lunch at one, during which we heard news broadcasts about fall of Canton—most distressing. Clinic began again at two with usual routine of cases, over 300 in all. Took daily hospital accounts at close of clinic. ... Next, drove to Huaian to see a sick woman. Back at 6:30—kept alert for sound of warplanes. Supper and immediately afterwards night rounds in women's surgical wards with cursory rounds in men's surgical and inspection of electric light plant. Home to read a little in an interesting book on exploration and then to bed.

Sutsien, the home of a neighbor mission station, soon fell to the Japanese, and Tsingkiangpu was threatened. A missionary described one of the first bombings of the area:

> I saw citizens running to the fields near the Bells. Soon we saw ten planes come into sight flying like wild geese. They broke up into groups and went to work. The sound was terrific as the bombs struck. I peered around the corner and saw [a bomber] come up from a power dive just beyond the Gieser house. There was machine gun fire and two tremendous explosions.
>
> Two days later twelve planes came. ... They formed a line west of the Grand Canal about fifteen hundred feet in the air and began dropping a number of bombs all at once. With the windows exploding, the plaster falling, and bricks

pounding on the roof, I thought my house was coming down on my head. The girls' school had a direct hit and Miss Hwang, the matron, was killed instantly, along with the gateman.

Over twenty wounded had been brought to the hospital. Dr. Bell said that all would recover except two—a little girl who had her arm blown off and an old man who died on the operating table.

Early in 1939, six bombers emptied their loads just outside Tsingkiangpu. Then two enormous blasts sounded and a canal bridge and the city electric plant exploded. Then suddenly Japanese soldiers were seen entering the city. Because they wanted to use the city as a command headquarters, they'd feinted to the north and drawn the Chinese military out of the city. Then they swept massive armored and cavalry forces around by an undefended flank to take the city from the south. Believing that God had intervened to protect and preserve lives, the missionaries took hope.[6]

From Shanghai, Jimmy tried to keep in touch with loved ones in the U.S. To his granddaughters Mary Abbott and Sophie he wrote newsy, amusing letters. In one letter he shared typical grandfatherly wisdom:

"I want you to make good on your winter exams if you have to break a hamstring to do it. But, remember, I would rather have you fail on everything rather than do anything that is the least bit unfair or dishonest. It is mighty easy to do it without really thinking about it or intending it. But if you [cheat], it's not only wrong, it is a black mark to you always for everyone who knows it."

Jimmy and Sophie received an entertaining letter from Margaret Sells, missionary in Haishou. Her mother had recently joined her on the field and was learning, to her chagrin, how much the Chinese culture differed from her own. Through Margaret, the mother asked a Chinese to guess her age. The Chinese answered that, judging from her hair, she was 50 but judging from her face—70. In a society that reveres old age, this was a very polite response.

Margaret stated, "The reason for my writing this letter is that I owe now just slightly under a hundred letters. Mother is studying the language but I won't say how long every day. The other day, callers came while I was away and all of her hitherto studied phrases deserted her except one, which unfortunately happened to be 'goodbye.' Still more unfortunate, the word had its usually expected effect."

She continued, "My language skill also has many limitations. One of the latest was a surprise in the shape of baked, sweet chestnuts. I told our young cook to bake some pears but the word for chestnut and pear is the same—only the tone being different. Evidently I used the wrong tone and we had chestnuts fixed just exactly as baked pears should have been."

The language problems reminded Margaret of a story she'd heard from another missionary. Apparently, the missionary was trying to tell the story of Samson's destruction of a lion. But a child in the class expressed great puzzlement at why Samson should be praised for such a thing. Upon a little investigation the teacher discovered that, though she'd used the correct word, the tone was all wrong, and she had extolled Samson's courage for killing an "unmentionable small creature that is sometimes found in the coiffure of the 'great unwashed.'"

As Sophie's health declined, Jimmy did his best to care for her. In correspondence, he warmly affirmed that he was honored to do so, since she had served him for so long.

There still exists a copy of a love note Jimmy gave to Sophie on their 50th wedding anniversary, only months before her death. Never a skilled typist, Jimmy struggled with an ornery, ancient typewriter, but beneath the inserted words, corrections, and uneven letters is a moving tribute. A portion reads: "I can't begin to tell you, my dear, how much happiness you have brought into my life and what a true wife you have been to me in every way. ... My love for you began the night at the seminary chapel as you came out—my first day at college—and it has grown deeper and become a part of the very fiber of my being during each of the years as they have passed."

Calvin Chao, the Chinese preacher nursed back to health by Sophie, made a last visit to see her. Now an evangelist, he shared of God's work and told her how much she meant to him. During a lull in their conversation, Sophie said weakly, "I look ugly, don't I?"

"No," Calvin said, "you look like an angel to me."

Before he left her that day, Calvin told her he wanted to write her biography in English so that people might know what great missionaries she and Jimmy were.

Tears appeared in her eyes, and she lay silent for a while, unable to speak. Finally she said, "Promise me you would never do that."

"Why shouldn't I?" asked Calvin.

"Don't let me steal God's glory," she said.

Calvin left the Grahams to begin an evangelistic trip into China's interior. Flooding bogged him down temporarily in Yunnan, and he took the opportunity to hold special meetings in the local churches. From there he planned to travel to Kunming for a two-month stay, where he would assist an area missionary. Then he hoped to go on to Szechwan, preaching the Gospel as he went. By this time, means of transportation had generally improved. There was a time when Chinese were buried in whatever spot a geomancer considered lucky. Railways would actually be dismantled if they were thought to disturb the spirits of the haphazardly placed corpses of the deceased. But at some point citizens had convinced themselves that the ancestors were now pleasantly accustomed to the noise of trains, and railroads crisscrossed the countryside.

Meanwhile, Sophie's condition was degenerating quickly. When she died in early 1940, her body was completely worn out from serving God, but her soul was as fresh and pure as ever. She was buried in the Bubbling Well Cemetery in Shanghai.

Jimmy hardly knew how to live without his strong life partner and spiritual ally. Sophie was such a woman of God that, even in her helplessness, there was a power about her. She had stood like a rock by his side for almost 50 years. Though many missed her deeply, only a few family and friends were able to attend her memorial and graveside service.

Many wrote to Uncle Jimmy during this period. James III wrote his father, "I was in the midst of writing one of my long epistles to you when the news came of the passing of precious Mother. We realize how lonely and lost you will feel but the joy of knowing of her release and joy in the presence of the Lord must mitigate it greatly. She had longed to go for some time. In fact, I never saw anyone who all through life, even in the comparative vigor of health, was so constantly ready and even eager to be with the Lord."

Jimmy's daughter Fanny wrote from Virginia, "I know what a terrific hole her going has left in your life, my lamb. No woman that ever lived had a more loving, compassionate, unselfish husband. I know you are missing, not only the invalid of recent years, but what she has been to you all your years together."

In his letter of sympathy, missionary W.H. Hudson didn't even attempt to quote Scripture to Jimmy: "You are too well versed in Scripture for me to quote any. I only suggest that those who loved and served Him here will 'serve Him' there and see His face."

The Reverend Maxey Smith also gave a meaningful tribute: "Aunt Sophie remains in my memory as a true worker for God and a devoted life to Him and her family. Her constant thought of others, her wide love and smile, her understanding, her use of the musical talents God had given ... will ever remain my picture of her."

One missionary rejoiced with Jimmy at Sophie's release with these wonderfully appropriate words:

"O think! To step on shore
And that shore Heaven;
To take hold of a hand,
And that God's hand;
To breathe a new air,
And find it celestial air;
To feel invigorated,
And to know it immortality;
O think! To pass from the storm
And the tempest;
To one unbroken calm;
To wake up,
And find it glory."[7]

The same friend wrote, "I love to think of what joy you have had those years that she has been sick, in ministering to her. You have so often written of how you thank God for them."

Another added, "Sophie was prepared for a prepared place. ... [S]he is now gazing into the face of the Savior she loved. Mel Trotter used to say that was all he wanted to do for his first thousand years up there."

Jimmy traveled back to the United States and stayed for a period with his son and family in Glendale, California. He had a charming personality and still had some of that old Virginia gentleman in him, along with a powerful dose of evangelistic fervor. So every afternoon he went to call on neighbors, one by one. When someone answered the door, he'd say, "Good afternoon, madam. My name is Graham. I was a missionary in China and I'm here visiting my son and daughter-in-law."

Then he'd joke with the kids and draw the adults into conversation, asking them about their family, their interests, their religion. If opportunity presented itself, he would share the Gospel with them.

Typical Californians—sophisticated, self-engrossed, private—

were taken aback by this friendly old man. Gradually he won their hearts. When he left Glendale to stay with his daughter Fanny and her family in Lexington, Virginia, the California neighbors said their farewells tearfully—he had become everyone's grandfather.

During his decades in China, Jimmy had also, in spirit, adopted many missionary kids. And when the young people left China to continue their education in the U.S., he prayed faithfully for them and stayed in contact, corresponding voluminously, even sending gifts when he was able.

One of those he loved dearly was Ruth Bell, who knew him her entire life as simply "Uncle Jimmy." A letter remains which she wrote to Uncle Jimmy while a student at Wheaton College in Illinois. Anticipating his return to the U.S., she submitted a request: "We are having a Missions Conference here and are so anxious to have you bring us a message. We'd love to have you tell of your first years in China—of the stonings and spittings, the long years of apparent fruitlessness, and your confidence that the battle was the Lord's. That always thrills me through and through."

Ruth had met a fellow student named Billy Graham. Billy fell for her right away and began asking her out. Soon he wrote his mother saying that he'd found the girl he was going to marry. Ruth enjoyed times with him, but was a little slower at coming around to Billy's way of thinking. She was very much her own person, and she also had to get used to the idea of perhaps ending up married to an evangelist instead of going as a single missionary to Tibet. But finally she was won over, and she and Billy planned a wedding in Montreat, North Carolina, for August 13, 1943. Uncle Jimmy was proud and elated when the couple asked him to conduct the wedding ceremony, and he looked forward to it.[8] Neither Uncle Jimmy nor Ruth knew God had other plans for him that would pre-empt officiating at this wedding.

Back in China, Calvin Chao had suffered serious wounds in an accident and was now in Kweiyang recovering. Earlier, he had passed through the North Jiangsu region in his travels and was impressed with the steady spiritual growth that had taken place upon the foundation laid by Jimmy, Sophie, and others, beginning before the turn of the century. He wrote, "It is such a thorough work—far more in advanced stages than any work in the interior."

It was now over two and a half years since Sophie's passing, and Jimmy still sorely missed her. He was 84 years old and seemingly in good health. In March, Jimmy's daughter Sophie was in Johnson City, Tennessee, with friends, and she invited her father down for a visit. Jimmy reunited with her on March 11, and they spent several very enjoyable weeks together.

On the morning of April 22, Jimmy awoke as usual but complained of feeling quite dizzy and uncomfortable. The doctor ordered several days of rest, which seemed to have little benefit. He had experienced several mini-strokes during the past 16 months but had always been able to regain his strength. This time was different.

On Friday, April 30, he experienced a severe stroke and lost the use of the limbs on his left side. Though his mind remained clear, he exhibited a slight slurring of speech. Sophie telephoned Fanny and summoned her to Johnson City. She immediately drove to Tennessee, and the three spent a wonderful evening together on May 1st. The next morning Jimmy suffered another stroke, and from that time until the following Sunday, he was unable to move at all. The only communication he could make was closing or opening his eyes in response to questions. Finally, on the afternoon of May 9, a Mother's Day, he left to join his Sophie and the innumerable company.

Jimmy and Sophie Graham were two individuals out of billions throughout history. They devoted 50 years to a giant nation in which they could reach only the minutest few out of multiplied millions. So what was their legacy? Did they waste five decades separated from relations in their beloved Virginia, seeing their own children and grandchildren sent away for many years at a time for schooling? Did they waste their lives spreading a Gospel that many Chinese have never wanted to hear, a message many still reject? The answer is no, resoundingly no. Their supreme motivation was always their deep love and gratefulness to Christ. A scrap of text was recently found in which Jimmy expressed this in words:

> All of humanity's sin was laid on Christ in those last few hours. The final result of sin is hell, where no one can see God. And the most terrible experience of all for Christ was the hiding of His Father's face from Him as he took on our sin. Jesus had taken all that went before quietly, but when this awful result of sin was visited upon him, it wrenched from him the cry, 'My God, my God, why hast thou forsaken me!' So, while we think of the human side of redemption: the eternal happiness and glory and sinlessness that is to be ours when we see God face to face, we must not fail for a moment to place first that which made it all possible: the unthinkable love, pure and simple. Because it was not for Himself but for those who had spent a lifetime of sinning against Him. Isn't it incomprehensible? 'Oh, for such love let rocks and hills their lasting silence break!' May the slight comprehension that we can have of it here lead us to dedicate our lives more fully to Him and consider that all we have is His, not only because He gave it to us but because of this unspeakable LOVE.

The Grahams' family legacy is remarkable. The couple's three children devoted a total of 84 years as missionaries in the Orient. Of their grandchildren, three devoted a total of 67 years to full-time ministry, 37 of those years in foreign missions. Of their great-grandchildren, five are in career Christian ministry, two of them serving in overseas missions.

Jimmy and Sophie's testimony has reached individuals all over the world—sometimes reaping unusual spiritual fruit. Mary, one of their granddaughters, once shared in a school about the Grahams' experiences during the Boxer Rebellion. Later she received a thank-you note from a sixth grader named Steve, who said the stories had greatly affected him. Many years later this same young man began making evangelistic trips to Japan. Today he is a church planter in Kobe, Japan. This is but one of many examples of the hundreds influenced indirectly by the Grahams.

For over 40 years after the Grahams left, China was closed to Western missionaries, but as author John Piper put it, "This is not because Jesus fell into a tomb. He stepped in. And when it was sealed over, He saved fifty million Chinese from inside—without Western missionaries. And when it was time, He pushed the stone away so we could see what He had done. When it looks like He is buried for good, Jesus is doing something awesome in the dark."[9]

During those decades, what was God accomplishing inexorably in North Jiangsu, the very region where the Grahams worked? As late as 1958, the Chinese Communists were proudly proclaiming the combined Huaiyin/Shuyang county a religionless region. But when Mary Graham Reid visited China in the late 1980s, she met a Pastor Hsieh in Shanghai. He had known Mary's father and had heard him preach, and through other Chinese, he had heard of Mary's grandparents. He'd been imprisoned for his faith for 23 years, treated severely. Repeatedly he was beaten, and his hands were kept behind his back—wrists bleeding from the tight metal bands. Because he received no medical treatment, the wrists became severely and chronically infected.

Though the pastor's face and body wore the marks of suffering, his face shone with the glory of God. When Mary marveled that he was able to survive the imprisonments, he repeated what the Apostle Paul said: "His grace is enough for me, therefore I will glory in my afflictions that his power may rest upon me" (cf. 2 Corinthians 12:9).

Pastor Hsieh introduced her to a woman who accompanied them to Tsingkiangpu. The mud wall that surrounded the city was gone, and it was difficult to identify old landmarks. Some old men were sitting by the canal, and when Mary asked them if they knew where her grandfather had lived, amazingly, they remembered and directed the party to the house. Though the old brick house was in ramshackle condition, Mary recognized it immediately.

She was taken to several homes where people passed on stories they'd been told of her grandparents, and a few also remembered her father's occasional ministry forays into the area.

Billy and Ruth Graham visited Tsingkiangpu in 1989 and found Jimmy and Sophie's former home being used as a grocery outlet. They had the opportunity to speak to various church leaders and learned details of the church in the region. There is a government-authorized Three-Self church, and all members must register with civil authorities. But the number of Christians not registered in the Three-Self church is far larger throughout China than the official number. A senior pastor of the Three-Self church told Billy and Ruth of 40,000–50,000 registered church members in Jiangsu and surrounding counties. However, a church administrator for the area said that there were believed to be over 300,000 Christians in the region.

When two Southern Presbyterian missionary children returned as adults to visit the Jiangsu region in 1994, there were no proper church buildings in what is now Huaiyin city (Tsingkiangpu). They were invited to speak at the regular Tuesday afternoon worship service meeting in the Graham's former missionary residence. They were told that about 1,000 people, the usual attendance, filled the house and porch and spacious courtyard. It was estimated that there were more than 400,000 Christians in the entire Huaiyin Prefecture, worshipping in 1,200 churches or private meeting points. Construction work had begun on what would be the largest church in Jiangsu Province. It was being built at a cost of over three million Yuan.[10]

As of April 2000, the seven-story Huai'an church was

completed, with a capacity of about 2,800. Today, the church in this region continues to grow steadily, and there is talk of building a 10,000-seat sanctuary on the freeway between Shanghai and Beijing, which passes right by the old Tsingkiangpu area.[11] The church that had been meeting in Uncle Jimmy and Aunt Sophie's former home in the 1990s has since converted the old building into a clinic for the poor.

Through the decades of Jimmy Graham's ministry, scattered here and there in his letters is a phrase which reflects his joyous amazement that, rising out of the many years of apparent fruitlessness, he and his associates were seeing thousands of Chinese in North Jiangsu courageously placing their faith in Christ. The phrase can be repeated by those who read the Grahams' remarkable story and all that has occurred since:

"What hath God wrought!"

Facing page: On their 50th wedding anniversary, days before his 76th birthday and only a few months before Sophie's death, Jimmy sat down in front of a borrowed, ancient typewriter to compose a love note. He struggled with typos, but beneath the inserted words, corrections, and uneven letters is a moving tribute.

October3rd 1889-9ctOber 3rd 1939

Sweetie   This is a big date with me,forty years ago you became mine own dear Wife
Wife-I could hardly believe my good fortune at the theearly date and I still
find it almost as hard to believe that it is true that have been mine all these
years-it seems too good to be true.I thank God for it everyday and many times a
day.Ic ant begin to tell you,My Dear,how much happiness you have brought into my
life and what a true wife you have been to me in every way.I simply cannot imagi
ine what these days and years would have been with your presence and love and
help
sympathy and sympathy in everyway . My love for you began that night at the
Seminary Chapel door as you came out-my first day at College,and it has grown
deeper and become a part of the very fiber of my being during each of the years
as they have passed.

MODERN-DAY CHURCH IN CHINA.

WORSHIPPERS FILL MODERN-DAY CHURCH IN THE AREA OF
CHINA WHERE UNCLE JIMMY AND AUNT SOPHIE SERVED.

MARY GRAHAM REID, GRANDDAUGHTER OF JIMMY GRAHAM II,
VISITED CHINESE CHRISTIANS IN TSINGKIANGPU
(NOW CALLED HUAIYIN) IN 1987.

James R. Graham III

FUTURE GENERATIONS WILL
ALSO SERVE HIM.
OUR CHILDREN WILL HEAR
ABOUT THE WONDERS OF THE LORD.
HIS RIGHTEOUS ACTS WILL BE TOLD
TO THOSE YET UNBORN.
THEY WILL HEAR ABOUT EVERYTHING
HE HAS DONE.

PSALM 22:30–31, NLT

AFTERWORD

"Son," Sophie said, "please don't play football."

Sixteen-year-old James R. Graham III was boarding a ship in Shanghai, leaving home for his father's alma mater, Hampden-Sydney College, in Virginia. With 196 pounds of muscle in a six foot package, Graham was a natural for the football team, but his mother gave her rationale that day: tennis was okay, or basketball, but in football he could sustain a crippling injury. And that would derail what she was convinced was God's plan for her athletic son, to serve God in China. After all, that's what she and her husband had already done for 25 years.

Jim Graham was welcomed by fellow students for his powerful tennis game, for his basketball prowess, but why wouldn't such a specimen play football? The answer, of course, was that his mother didn't want him to. This naturally led to unbearable ragging about "mommy's little patsy." Finally he persuaded his mother to change her mind. Her fears were unfounded, for he came through unscathed, and his dreams were fulfilled, as the young Graham smashed his way into local football legend.

His reputation was such that, upon graduation, when he joined the Marines to help finish off World War I, instead of sending him off to combat as he intended, they put him on the Marine football team! Following military service, he was not headed to China to serve God, as his mother had so long hoped and prayed, but headed in the opposite direction, to use his towering physical and mental strength to serve Jim Graham. He wrote political speeches for friends, played semi-pro football, and became engaged to a girl named Louise.

Here's how it happened. Back during college days, one afternoon he and some football buddies were strolling into town and just "happened" to pass through the campus of State Teachers' College, a women's school. Jim Graham was stopped dead in his tracks. He heard the voice of an angel floating down from a second story window. "Wow! I've got to meet that girl."

"No doubt a whopper," said one of his friends, "Most people with that kind of voice aren't much to look at." But the next day in church he and his friends were astonished to hear the same voice, and before them stood, not an angel, but a beautiful co-ed, singing the same hymn that had so mesmerized him the day before. They met that day, and a lifetime later at Louise's funeral, her daughter Sophie sang that hymn:

> Glory to thee, my God, this night
> For all the blessings of the light.
> Keep me, oh, keep me, King of kings
> Beneath thine own almighty wings.
>
> Teach me to live, that I might dread
> The grave as little as my bed;
> Teach me to die, that so I may
> Rise glorious at the Judgment Day. [1]

But after military service Jim Graham must have forgotten about that Judgment Day, for he was in hot pursuit of his own interests. Things were going his way till one day he made a big mistake. Sundays were usually spent on the tennis court, but he wanted a friend to "hear a real Protestant preacher," so he broke his customary date with the tennis court and went to church. On that fateful Sunday they heard the Reverend Tolley Thompson preach as fine a sermon as Graham had ever heard. He later reported:

> Dr. Thompson described a hypothetical young man who had been taught to pray and honor God. He said, "Maybe his father was a pastor, or maybe even his parents were missionaries. They wanted him to be a preacher, but he began to veer away from the Lord." It sounded as if he had been reading my mail. I was sure somebody had tipped him off and that it was a deliberate set-up.
>
> He said, "This young man sold his birthright for a mess of pottage." After he had said it the third time I said to myself, "Whether or not he is saying it deliberately, it's the truth. The cap fits."

Graham returned to his little room and fell to his knees, weeping his way to repentance and committing his life to God for China, which he then called "my people." He was 23 years old. Fearful of what his fiancé's response would be, Graham hesitated to share this life-transforming decision. The story continues in his own words:

> I was engaged to a beautiful girl, Louise, and I told her, "I have made a deal with God. I'm not going to a theological seminary, I'm going to the mission field to make Christ known. That's what's in my heart." Louise looked at me, tears rolled down her cheeks and she began laughing. She said, "That's what we have been praying for all the time."
>
> "Who is 'we'?" I asked.
>
> "Your mother and I. We have had a compact and have asked the Lord to turn your heart back."

Thus it was that China was to feel the impact of the gifted son of illustrious parents. Driven by the same vision, passion, and indomitable courage, he—like them—was to tirelessly evangelize the people of China. But there were other legacies from his parents. In those early days of the younger Graham's ministry, his father, surviving the hostility of a resistant people, was waging a parallel battle, this one against liberalism in his own sending agency. Thus "separation" from unbelief became a dominant, lifelong theme of the younger Graham as well. In those days he was greatly influenced by the famed China pioneer missionary, Robert A. Jaffray, who emphasized the second coming of Christ. This also became a major theme of Graham's ministry.

But something was lacking. He was a successful evangelist, a master of the Chinese language—it was rumored that he knew the classics better than many Chinese scholars. But where was the spiritual power he longed for? He had heard of revival fires sweeping across interior China, which seemed to evidence a spiritual vitality he longed to personally experience. He toyed with the idea of traveling to investigate but hesitated. The spark of this movement was a Norwegian Baptist and Graham was a North American Presbyterian. There was more, however. The revivalist was a woman, and Graham didn't believe in women preachers. But he finally became desperate enough to humble himself and take the long train journey to the current place Marie Monson was holding forth. The first night, in the packed-out tent, she spoke from the Ten Commandments. "Fair enough," thought Graham, "they can use a dose of law." The second night she was back in Exodus 20, and by the third night, Graham had enough. At the end of the service he sought out the diminutive evangelist and, towering over her, thundered, "Miss Monson, when will you leave the somber legalisms of the Old Testament to the ancient people to whom they were addressed and nourish us with the grace of Calvary?"

"Mr. Graham," Monson replied, "until the ears of the heart have been opened with the thunders of Sinai they cannot even hear the sweet grace notes of Calvary."

This brief encounter was to mark James R. Graham III from then on. Merely preaching truth would not suffice. Spirit-energized practical holiness became a hallmark of his life and ministry.

Then came the invasion of China. The Japanese were in; the missionaries were out, including James III and his wife with their three daughters and two sons. Back home in the U.S., it was no trick to line up speaking engagements, given his personal charisma, his powerful concepts, and his sheer eloquence. He was assisted in arranging those engagements by a young woman, another Louise. Of her we shall hear more. But during those "in-between" years, one year stands out above all others in terms of long-range impact, the 1939–40 school year.

Wheaton College gave Graham an honorary doctorate, so from then on he became "Doctor Jim" to his eager disciples. Wheaton also invited him to teach a survey course of the Bible. Rumor has it that his "survey" course never got beyond Genesis 6! Doubtless a true rumor, for Graham believed the seedbed of all Bible truth lay embedded in those chapters. The astonishing thing, however, is the outcome of that single class.

When Graham entered a room, electricity seemed to crackle. It must have jumped the spark to many a life, for all, including some destined for fame in the Christian world, sat mesmerized for that year. For example, there were the "Three Musketeers," as Graham fondly dubbed them: Donald Hoke, distinguished educator, Kenneth Hansen, founder of ServiceMaster, and professional magician Phil Foxwell, who married the Wheaton president's daughter and served for decades in Japan. Also sitting under his spell was Ruth Bell, daughter of the Grahams' longtime colleague in China, Doctor L. Nelson Bell. All testified in later years that Dr. Jim was a powerful molding influence in life and ministry.

Perhaps the greatest impact of that year was through the Ruth

Bell connection. The year following, after Dr. Jim and family had headed west toward an anticipated return to China, another Graham, unrelated, enrolled at Wheaton. Before long, Billy Graham caught Ruth Bell, if not the other way around, and with her came plenty of "Dr. Jim" stories. Billy's own family back in North Carolina had long known about the missionary ministry of the "Grahams of China"—Uncle Jimmy, the father, and Dr. Jim, the son. But Ruth introduced Billy to a full dose of "Uncle Jimmy" and "Dr. Jim" lore. Thus a lifelong mentoring relationship was begun.

For example, when the young Billy Graham had his first big break in the tent "cathedral" at Los Angeles' Washington and Hill Streets Crusade, he wasn't prepared for the Crusade to continue on for eight weeks. He ran out of sermon material, he says, and in desperation called on Dr. Jim to supply the lack. A half century later Billy Graham was to testify that he thought often and fondly of Dr. Jim, "especially when I use his sermons!" It would be hard to measure the impact of that single year of ministry at Wheaton College, when a band of eager disciples caught the fire and spread it across the nations for more than half a century.

At the end of that school year, Graham received an invitation from General and Madame Chiang Kai-shek to return to China and preach the Gospel to the new recruits of the Chinese Nationalist Army. The war with the invading Japanese raged on, and Chiang Kai-shek's other war against the Communist insurgents was not going well. The Generalissimo was pressed in a giant pincer between Communists and the Japanese. The president of the Republic of China, encouraged by his committed Christian wife, felt his troops needed spiritual reinforcement. So it was that Graham boarded the China-bound ship alone, leaving his wife and smaller children at home. He had no sooner steamed out under the Golden Gate Bridge, however, than the ship u-turned and headed back to harbor. It was December 7, 1941.

At the time Graham did not know that his eldest son, James Graham IV, stationed on a ship at Pearl Harbor, had just come under attack. When the elder Graham arrived home, he received word from the Navy that his son had been killed along with the thousands who lost their lives that epochal day. It isn't hard to imagine the depths of grief James III and Louise experienced. A few days later, however, a correction came: Their Jimmy had been injured, not killed. Patriot that he was, James R. Graham IV continued in the Navy till retirement.

Dreams for returning to China having been forcibly set aside, Graham began what was to become a decade of ministry in Southern California, publishing a privately circulated journal, writing books, and, especially, forming a little church called Olivet House. In truth, however, he was forming another generation of disciples.

It was in this large house-converted-to-meeting-place that he preached, taught, and mentored dozens of mostly young adults. The newcomer might wonder that such a group would sit spellbound for a sermon of more than an hour on Sunday morning, surprised when Graham would announce midsermon that it was time for lunch. The newcomer—but not the veteran—might also be surprised that the abrupt ending was a mirage. The sermon would be concluded in an exceedingly lengthy closing prayer!

It was through hearing Graham preach that one of those disciples, Navy man John Reid, met Graham's oldest daughter, Mary. Together they served God with great effectiveness for over three decades in Japan. It was during those Olivet years that Graham also made champion tennis players out of his two youngest, Louise and Tucker. They were the only two of Graham's five who caught the "tennis bug," at least a heavy enough dose to reach the top. Louise claims her regimen was two hours a day of practice with lots of coaching from famous pros lined up by her father, and from her own dad himself. Of course, more important to her father than tennis, than hard-driving competition, than winning, was teaching the Word. So, says she, that's what Louise got on the long trip to and from the Los Angeles Tennis Club! That foundation in the Word was to prove essential in years to come when she served God with her pastor husband.

It was also during those days that Graham's patient, loving wife Louise finished her course. She had never been of robust health, but gave what limited strength she had to love her family and others well. And she was well-loved by all who knew her, and especially by her husband. The grief was great, but now he was free to return to his beloved people.

It wasn't just his own inner compulsion, however. Chiang Kai-shek, now exiled to the island of Formosa, still wanted Graham to return. This time the Generalissimo wanted help in educating the youth of Taiwan. So it was that Graham, at age 57, when most begin to think of shuffleboard in Florida, not only continued to overwhelm opponents on the tennis courts but also set about forming a Christian university. In 1955, he established the College of Science and Engineering and long before it was ready to operate, 1,500 students were beating on the doors, seeking admission. His school met with instant success but also quickly got away from him. His vision was a Christian college, modeled after the liberal arts college at Wheaton, where he had taught almost two decades earlier, but the organizational structure was such that control soon shifted to others. The Chinese educational leaders who took charge didn't have Graham's vision of a thoroughly Christian university. So Graham, typically, went out after a new vision. This time it was to be more like a Bible college, training for ministry. In later years Graham liked to say, "The first school was my Leah, but Christ's College became my Rachel."

He had long been a friend of Robert C. McQuilkin, first president of Columbia Bible College. In fact, his two younger daughters attended there, Sophie for a degree and Louise for a husband! And it was at the college's summer retreat center in the North Carolina mountains that he met Sarah, manager of Ben Lippen Conference Center. One who was present when Graham's eye first lighted on Sarah Chapel testified she saw the flame ignite at that moment. They married, and Sarah was to be his loyal help during most of the years of his Taiwan sojourn as an educator.

When Sarah finished her course, God provided the aging Graham with a lifetime friend, another Louise. This was the Louise who worked with Graham in the 1930s during his itinerant preaching days in America. It was from him she caught the vision of mission work in China. She went as a single missionary, later marrying a China missionary. She and her husband were eventually forced out by the Communist takeover, but they then had a significant ministry among the Chinese in Tokyo for many years. Much later, when her husband died, God knew James Graham needed another gracious, loving partner for the last lap of the journey. God gave him this second Louise when he was 80 years of age! But back to the story.

In 1959, the doors opened at Christ's College. Graham had discovered a beautiful location for the campus atop a hill near Taipei, overlooking the Tamsui River. This time he wasn't going to turn it over to someone else to deflect his purposes. He himself would preside. But at 61 how long could he preside? Astonishingly, for 23 years! This was to be his legacy, his greatest contribution to his beloved China, as hundreds of young people spread out across the world with James R. Graham's vision of Spirit-filled living and passionate evangelism.

Graham was nothing if not authoritarian—in his preaching, in his teaching, and in his administration of a college. But there are two reasons young people accepted this, and loved him in it, some near to idolatry. For such an imposing intellect and physical presence, he could have been arrogant or unapproachable. But even teens found him startlingly humble—eager to listen, quick to designate you a "prince." Among the Chinese, however, there was another reason for their eager acceptance of his benign autocracy— age is greatly honored, wisdom of the ancients extolled, and authority respected. So they came, hundreds of them, year after year, to sit at his feet, even when he could no longer stand.

Without doubt, illustrious though his varied contributions to the Cause may have been, Christ's College was the grandest, a truly remarkable finale. But Graham never rested on his newspaper clippings, he never stopped dreaming. Listen to one of his dreams, written once Christ's College was well-launched:

> My sense of obligation goes beyond Taiwan, for God has burdened me with all of Southeast Asia. I am thinking of thousands of islands in Indonesia where the people have never been reached with the Gospel. Do you know what I would like to do? I would like to charter a Chinese ship in Keelung and fit it out with young missionaries and doctors and dentists, and spend months sailing from island to island, spreading the news of Christ's salvation.

Graham was 76 years of age!

When James R. Graham III died on June 18, 1982, at 84 years of age, the pallbearers, his graduates, all of whom he considered his own "children," donned dark glasses. Son-in-law John Reid wanted to know why. To hide the tears, these grown men explained. James R. Graham III was deeply loved.

When Jimmy and Sophie Graham left the Shenandoah Valley of Virginia for China in 1889, who could have calculated the eternal impact of their service, spanning over a half century. To bring thousands to the Savior and gather many of those into 38 new churches, to build hospitals and schools throughout northern China, and to mentor hundreds of Chinese Christian leaders would have been legacy enough. Who could have predicted then that one of their greatest and most lasting contributions to the Chinese people would be a son, James R. Graham III?

AFTERWORD CONTRIBUTED BY J. ROBERTSON McQUILKIN

THE GRAHAM FAMILY

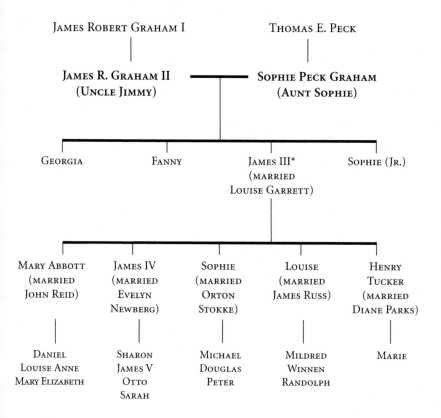

JAMES ROBERT GRAHAM I

THOMAS E. PECK

JAMES R. GRAHAM II
(UNCLE JIMMY)

SOPHIE PECK GRAHAM
(AUNT SOPHIE)

GEORGIA   FANNY   JAMES III*
(MARRIED
LOUISE GARRETT)
    SOPHIE (JR.)

MARY ABBOTT
(MARRIED
JOHN REID)

JAMES IV
(MARRIED
EVELYN
NEWBERG)

SOPHIE
(MARRIED
ORTON
STOKKE)

LOUISE
(MARRIED
JAMES RUSS)

HENRY
TUCKER
(MARRIED
DIANE PARKS)

DANIEL
LOUISE ANNE
MARY ELIZABETH

SHARON
JAMES V
OTTO
SARAH

MICHAEL
DOUGLAS
PETER

MILDRED
WINNEN
RANDOLPH

MARIE

*After Louise's death, James III married Sarah Chapel; after Sarah's death, James III married Louise Reike Hunter.

ENDNOTES

Dedication:

1. From the hymn "The Son of God Goes Forth to War" (1827), by Reginald Heber.

Introduction:

1. From the hymn "O Zion Haste" (1870), words by Mary Ann Faulkner Thomson 1834–1923, music by James Walch 1837–1901.
2. David Aikman, *Jesus in Beijing: How Christianity Is Transforming China and Changing the Global Balance of Power* (Washington D.C.: Regnery Publishing, 2003), 291.
3. From "O Zion Haste" (1870).

Chapter 1:

1. Jack Lynch, "St. George Tucker Americanizes Sir William Blackstone," *Colonial Williamsburg* (Spring 2003): 83–84.
2. Beverley D. Tucker, and Percy Turrentine, *Nathaniel Beverley Tucker: Prophet of the Confederacy 1784–1851* (Tokyo: Nan'un-Do, 1979).
3. Robert Woodworth, *A History of the Presbyterian Church in Winchester, Virginia, 1780–1949* (Winchester, Va.: Piper Printing, 1950), 39.
4. Ibid.
5. Henry Tucker Graham, *The Old Manse* (Richmond, Va.: Whittet & Shepperson, 1915), 1.

6. James Graham, "Some Reminiscences," (n.p., n.d.).

7. James Graham, "Stonewall Jackson: The Man, the Soldier, the Christian," (n.p., n.d.).

8. James Robertson, Jr., *Stonewall Jackson: The Man, the Soldier, the Legend* (New York: Simon & Schuster, 1997), 324.

9. Ibid., 323.

10. From private correspondence from Fanny Graham to Mrs. Stonewall Jackson, 31 December 1863.

11. From private correspondence from Mrs. Stonewall Jackson to Fanny Graham, 20 July 1863.

12. From private correspondence from Fanny Graham to Mrs. Stonewall Jackson, 20 June 1863.

13. Richard France, "Henry Martyn," in *Five Pioneer Missionaries* (Carlisle, Pa.: Banner of Truth, 1965), 277.

14. Ibid., 298.

15. Ibid., 262–263.

16. Douglas Kelly, *Preachers with Power* (Carlisle, Pa.: Banner of Truth, 1992), 68.

17. C. R. Vaughn, "Biographical Sketch of Dr. T. E. Peck," *Union Seminary Magazine* 12 (March/April 1894).

18. Ibid.

Chapter 2:

1. "The Grand Canal of China," *South China Morning Post*, 1985. (Specific date and pages unknown.)

2. John Pollock, *A Foreign Devil in China: The Story of Dr. L. Nelson Bell* (Minneapolis: World Wide Publications, 1971), 42.

3. *Columbia Encyclopedia*, 6th ed., s.v. "Opium War" and "Sino-Japanese War."

4. J. Buschini, *The Boxer Rebellion* (Lawrence, Mass.: Small Planet Communications, 2000), 2–4.

5. Edward Bliss, Jr., *Beyond the Stone Arches* (New York: John Wiley and Sons, 2001), 89.

6. G. Thompson Brown, *Earthen Vessels and Transcendent Power: American Presbyterians in China, 1837–1952* (New York: Orbis, 1997), 156.

7. Ruth Graham, "The Executioner," in *Legacy of a Pack Rat* (Nashville: Thomas Nelson, 1989). This entire story is adapted from Ruth Graham's true account in the book *Legacy of a Pack Rat*.

Chapter 3:

1. Christina Yuan, *Biography of Dr. James R. Graham III*, trans. John C. Wang (n.p., n.d.), 6–7.
2. Ibid., 7.
3. Ibid., 4.
4. *Columbia Encyclopedia*, 6th ed., s.v. "Sun Yat-sen."

Chapter 4:

1. Pollock, *Foreign Devil in China*, 36, 43–44.
2. Ibid., 54–55.
3. Ibid., 154.
4. Ken and Kay Gieser, *Ken and Kay Gieser: 1930–1981*, (n.p., n.d.), 91. (self-published autobiography)
5. Pollock, *Foreign Devil in China*, 76–77.
6. Ibid., 65.

Chapter 5:

1. Gieser, *Ken and Kay Gieser*, 54.
2. Pollock, *Foreign Devil in China*, 51.

Chapter 6:

1. Gieser, *Ken and Kay Gieser*, 190.

Chapter 7:

1. Pollock, *Foreign Devil in China*, 128–129.
2. Patricia Cornwell, *Ruth, A Portrait: The Story of Ruth Bell Graham* (New York: Doubleday, 1997), 17–18, 23.
3. Gieser, *Ken and Kay Gieser*, 174–175.
4. Ibid., 200–201.
5. Pollock, *Foreign Devil in China*, 46.

Chapter 8:

1. Gieser, *Ken and Kay Gieser*, 82.
2. Cornwell, *Ruth, A Portrait*, 34–35.

3. Gieser, *Ken and Kay Gieser*, 207.

Chapter 9:

1. Cornwell, *Ruth, A Portrait*, 34.
2. *Rethinking Missions: A Layman's Inquiry After 100 Years* (New York: Harper & Brothers, 1932).
3. Pollock, *Foreign Devil in China*, 143–144, 146.
4. Ibid., 204–206.
5. Gieser, *Ken and Kay Gieser*, 192–193.
6. Ibid., 98–103.
7. Ibid., 97.
8. Ibid., 149.
9. Ibid., 203–204.
10. Pollock, *Foreign Devil in China*, 273.

Chapter 10:

1. Paul Frankenstein, "The Birth of Modern China," in *Condensed China* [online], [cited 24 Oct. 2005]; available from http://asterius.com/china/china4.html.
2. Ken Curtis et al., "Betty and John Stam: Young Missionaries Martyred," no. 160, *Glimpses* (Worcester: Christian History Institute, 2003).
3. Carl Stam, presentation during Hymn Service "Martyrs of the Faith," Southern Baptist Theological Seminary, Louisville, Ky., 4 Feb. 2003, [online] [cited 24 Oct. 2005]; available from http://www.carlstam.org/Stam_Family_Heritage/JohnandBetty.doc.
4. Gieser, *Ken and Kay Gieser*, 105.
5. Ibid., 81–82.
6. Pollock, *Foreign Devil in China*, 264.
7. Origin uncertain. Some sources attribute the poem to Robert E. Selle.
8. Pollock, *Foreign Devil in China*, 299–300.
9. John Piper, *A Godward Life: Savoring the Supremacy of God in All Life*, vol. 2 (Salem, Ore.: Multnomah, 2001). 124.
10. Brown, *Earthen Vessels*, 306.
11. From letter written about current Chinese church to John and Mary Reid, 28 February 2005.

Afterword

1. From the hymn "All Praise to Thee My God This Night" (ca. 1674), words by Thomas Ken.

*Every effort has been made to give proper credit to other authors. If there are cases in which this has been overlooked, please inform the author so that future reprints will contain appropriate changes.

BIBLIOGRAPHY

Frankenstein, Paul. "The Birth of Modern China." In *Condensed China* [online]. [cited 24 Oct. 2005]. Available from http://asterius.com/china/china4.html.

Vaughan, C. R. "Biographical Sketch of Dr. T.E. Peck." *Union Seminary Magazine* 12 (March/April 1894).

Buschini, J. *The Boxer Rebellion.* Lawrence, Mass.: Small Planet Communications, 2000.

Cornwell, Patricia. *Ruth, A Portrait: The Story of Ruth Bell Graham.* New York: Doubleday, 1997.

Graham, Ruth Bell. *Footprints of a Pilgrim: The Life and Loves of Ruth Bell Graham.* Nashville: Word Books, 2001.

France, Richard. "Henry Martyn." In *Five Pioneer Missionaries.* Carlisle, Pa.: Banner of Truth, 1965.

Graham, Henry T. *The Old Manse.* Richmond: Whittet & Shepperson, 1915.

Graham, Ruth. "The Executioner." In *Legacy of a Pack Rat.* Nashville: Thomas Nelson, 1989.

Kelly, Douglas. *Preachers with Power.* Carlisle, Pa.: Banner of Truth, 1992.

Pollock, John. *A Foreign Devil in China: The Story of Dr. L. Nelson Bell.* Minneapolis: World Wide Publications, 1971.

Robertson, James, Jr. *Stonewall Jackson: The Man, the Soldier, the Legend.* New York: Simon & Schuster, 1997.

*The majority of material for this volume is drawn from a private collection of well over 200 letters written by and to James II and Sophie Graham. Approximately 103 of these letters were written by Graham family members between 1916 and 1939. The hundreds of references taken from these letters are not footnoted.

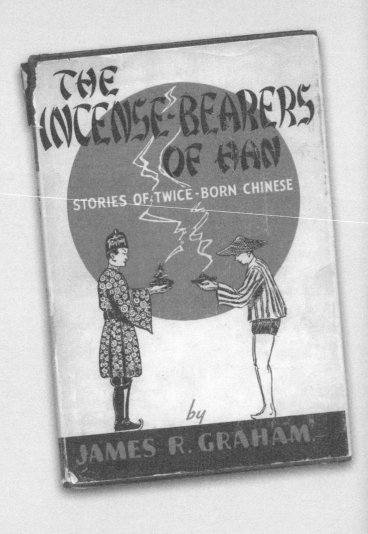

CONVERSION STORIES FROM CHINA

The following stories were told by James R. Graham III. They were published in a slightly different form in 1941 under the title *The Incense-Bearers of Han: Stories of Twice-Born Chinese* (Grand Rapids: Zondervan). A photograph of the dust cover of the 1941 book, which has been out of print for many years, is shown at left.

THE TIGER BECOMES A LAMB

Mr. Wang is the third brother in that particular family of Wang which dwells in the village of Wang in the northern reaches of the province of Kiangsu. He is a large man, about six feet in height, with broad shoulders and a sizeable head. His wide flat nose is fairly well distributed over the area of his face, which is somewhat reminiscent of a meat platter.

After arising at a late hour of the morning and inhaling his morning ration of soft rice or wheat gruel, he sweeps majestically and importantly down the street, hands in his sleeves, to the village tea shop. There, with legs crossed, and jerking the up-pointed toe to the cadence of the melody, he listens to an itinerant bard chant the sagas of his people while fondling his tea cup with his strong, well-shaped fingers. Time is no object, and Mr. Wang remains at his table long after the transient songster has taken his departure.

Presently he is joined by a group of friends who are in turn served tea by the noisy and loquacious attendant who greets the newcomers familiarly. This hearty man represents a type–numerous, distinctive, and interesting. He wears a well-worn satin gown and is girded about the waist with an apron that flows well-nigh down to the hem of his garment, caked with the grease and wipings of the years. Over his shoulder is slung a cotton rag that was probably white in the Tang Dynasty, but not since. At a jaunty angle on the top of his head rests the conventional small hat, battered and shiny with grease and surmounted by a frayed cloth button, which peeps through its insulation of red silk thread.

He places a pot with a thin sprinkling of tea leaves over the bottom, and a cup in front of each of the patrons, then swaggers over to the stove in the corner from which he takes a kettle with an amazingly long spout. With his left hand he grasps the tea pot, tilts it over, and thumbs aside the cover which is about the size of a silver dollar. Then, from a distance of not less than two feet, he propels a stream of boiling water squarely into the aperture in the top of the pot. If the dexterity of his right hand should fail him, he would have a couple of scalded fingers on his left!

After the usual amenities, Mr. Wang sits phlegmatically listening to his friends discuss money, local politics, the crops, and bandit situation, and the doings of the townspeople. The content of the conversation of these ... wiseacres does not differ greatly from that of the casual meetings of mid-morning Coca-Cola drinkers at the fountains along America's Main Street. This difference, however, is to be noted: The wise men of the East are vastly more leisurely and less hurried, and their materialism is freely interspersed with philosophical observations and platitudes, and clothed with a degree of sanctimoniousness by a multitude of proverbial and classical quotations.

Finally aroused from his silence, our Mr. Wang feels called upon to enlighten his friends with pearls of his wisdom and observation. He uncrosses his legs, plants both feet on the mud floor, pulls up his bench, extends both arms, flicks back each sleeve with a swift motion of the opposite hand, and proceeds to expatiate. With numerous gesticulations and facial grimaces, he delivers himself of what he, at least, believes to be the final word on every topic.

He expresses deep distress at the degeneracy of the government both provincial and local, and deplores the general departure from the economic principles of the philosopher Mencius. The youth he avers to be growing up as barbarians uninstructed in the lofty moral precepts of the sage Confucius, inducing misgovernment of all kinds and official rapacity even to the extent of connivance with banditry. Otherwise (with lowered voice and furtive side-glances) how could the Tiger be permitted to continue his nightly depredations? His auditors all grunt assent, as one puts in, "Did you hear that night before last, that pock-marked one raided the Chang family village? Who knows when it will be the turn of our village? Our only hope is that he will respect the ancestral name. I am told the chieftain is himself of the name of Wang even as are we."

"Yes, yes," agreed the others, "they call him Wang-Three, the Tiger!"

After a little altercation as to who will pay for the tea, our friend Mr. Wang lifts his long gown from the bottom, projects his fingers into his belt pouch and extracts some copper coins. With a toss of his right hand to arrange them for counting, he jerks his right thumb nail three times to deftly transfer three groups of five to his left hand, which he lays on the table. He throws a couple more down as a tip for the waiter and they all make their departure. Mr. Wang, the stalwart one, saunters slowly up the narrow village street, hands in his sleeves and a chuckle in his heart. Little did they dream that the pious propounder of the teachings of the sages by day was Wang-Three, the Tiger, himself.

I was going to preach the Gospel and teach the Word of God in the Market-Village-of-the-Great-Prosperity. Before leaving the city, a friend had told me, "There is a keen group of Christians in the town to which you're going, and the preacher, Mr. Wang, is an interesting character. Ask him to tell you his story if you have a chance."

I had been there two days when preacher Wang suggested that we walk over to a neighboring village for some visiting and street preaching. As we plodded down the dusty road, I said, "Mr. Wang, tell me your story. I would like to know how you came to be a Christian and a preacher of Christ's Gospel." Without hesitation he proceeded to do so. Stopping in the middle of the road he swept his arm around the horizon in a wide semi-circle.

"All over this country I was formerly known as Wang-Three the Tiger (Wang-San Lao-Hu), the chieftain over a robber band of about three hundred men. My home was in the Wang family village just a few li from the Chess-Board Village where you, pastor, were preaching just a few days ago." With this, he pointed in a northwesterly direction.

"By day I was a Confucian scholar and a respected citizen of my village, one of the elders in fact. By night I would join my men in some previously agreed upon rendezvous and lead them in a raid upon some village or town that we felt sure we could overpower. We would make a surprise attack concertedly upon three gates if it was a walled village, and when we had effected an entrance, would rob, kidnap, burn, and kill at will. Our methods were those of terrorists, and the vengeance we wreaked on any who dared to resist was awful. I recall one man who attempted to withstand me one night with a farming implement. I whirled up my broadsword to the height and split him in two from the crown of his head to his crotch, just as if he had been a piece of kindling wood."

No longer a young man, his eye was hardly yet dimmed or his natural force abated, and he was still able to give a convincing dramatization of bringing the broadsword down on the pate of his luckless victim. As the story progressed and he projected himself mentally back to the days of yore, his normally placid countenance darkened and his black eyes gleamed with some of the old fury. One felt inclined to breathe a prayer of thankfulness for having been kept from his path in those bold, bad days.

"I broke all of the Ten Commandments, some of them daily. I feared neither God nor man and became utterly hardened in sin, as this career of cruelty extended over several years."

By day one of the village gentry, and by night the roaring Tiger, this "elusive pimpernel" of old Cathay performed his dual role undiscovered and even unsuspected by his nearest neighbors.

And it came to pass on a certain day, strolling with his accustomed dignity down the main street of the Village of Wang, he approached the end of the street which terminated at the unimposing gate in the mud wall. On his left was a two-leafed door standing ajar and opening into a courtyard, on the far side of which was the usual mud structure with thatched roof, perhaps a little longer than most.

Mr. Wang had passed this same door innumerable times before and had seen the three bold characters, *"Yesu T'ang"* [Jesus Hall], inscribed over the entrance but had disdained to enter a place where his mercenary countrymen were employed by the "men from the ocean" to preach some strange foreign doctrine, he knew not what.

On this occasion, seeking relief from the boredom of the languid village, his feet were arrested as the sounds of melody issuing from the inner temple lighted upon his ears. The melody was somewhat discordant to be sure, but differed in quality from that of the tea shop singers sufficiently to intrigue his imagination. What could they mean by those strange words?

Precious name, Oh, how sweet,

Hope of earth and joy of heaven.

He finally yielded to the inclination to go in and try to discover what it was all about. Just as he took his seat on one of the backless benches in the rear of the hall, the singing came to an end and a clean-cut looking young man stood up and opened a book and commenced to read. The reading was in the colloquial style of writing for which the classically trained Mr. Wang felt a contempt as being beneath the literary dignity of the scholar, but he found himself listening in spite of it. The story seemed to be about some Man who was led out to be crucified and of others crucified with Him.

The reading soon ceased and the young man with eloquent earnestness began to tell in his own words the story. He elucidated how this Righteous One, Yesu, had been led out to his crucifixion and that there were two robbers executed at the same time.

"Oh, they were robbers," thought Mr. Wang, "I never got that the first time."

Then the young man showed how one scoffed at Him and railed upon Him and was consigned as a result to eternal perdition, while the other by a simple act of faith had called upon Him and was promised an immediate entrance into Paradise. He went on to extol the grace of

God in Christ which extended to a robber and murderer full forgiveness and Paradise happiness on the sole condition of faith in this crucified Yesu and calling on His name. Works were definitely excluded since both his hands and his feet were nailed up.

"Truly that was a strange doctrine," thought the Tiger, "a robber like myself admitted to Paradise just by calling on the name of this Jesus!"

The simple message was concluded, and the little group who were present were urged to avail themselves of the free grace of Christ as did the penitent thief, lest having rejected it, they should be cast into the lake of fire as was the impenitent one.

Wang-San Lao-Hu, hardened sinner that he was, felt himself strangely warmed and interested. After the prayer of dismissal, he made his way forward and sought an opportunity to speak to the preacher.

Addressing the youthful minister he said, "Did I understand that the robber who was crucified with Jesus actually entered into Paradise?"

"Yes, sir, that is correct. That very day he joined Jesus in Paradise," came the reply.

"Do you think your Jesus could save me?"

"Indeed He can, sir." The preacher glowed with blessed assurance.

"Ah, but young man, you have no idea who I am."

"I admit, sir, that I don't know who you are, but if He could save a wicked robber, He can save a gentleman like yourself, whoever or whatever you are."

"Step over into this corner," ordered the big man.

The younger man obeyed. Casting a stealthy glance around, as if not caring to be overheard, Mr. Wang's face clouded with a scowl, and he placed his index finger on the apex of his nose, glared at the young preacher and rasped in a coarse whisper, "*Woa sz Wang-San Lao-Hu!*–I am Wang-Three-the-Tiger."

It was now the beloved young Timothy's turn to change expression. He paled perceptibly as he glanced toward the windows and door, expecting to see an influx of the "pock-marked ones" composing the Tiger's following.

"Do not be afraid. None of my men are here. But do you think your Jesus would receive Wang-San Lao-Hu?"

The messenger of the King gulped hard and strove to regain his composure. "Yes, yes, Mr. Wang. Certainly! Though your sins be as scarlet, they shall be white as snow, though they be red like crimson, they shall be as wool."

"What must I do about it?" inquired the Tiger.

"Just kneel here with me, and give your heart to Christ, for God's Word says, 'Whosoever shall call upon the name of the Lord, the same shall be saved.'"

Down on their knees they went together as the devout young preacher poured out his heart to God for the salvation of a lost soul.

We are back on the dusty road twenty years later as the erstwhile Tiger with some emotion concludes the story.

"And then, pastor, when he had prayed so earnestly and my heart was bent in repentance and conviction, he led me in a few petitions as I called on the Lord for His forgiveness and salvation. A flood of joy and peace came into my soul as the Holy Spirit came into me to dwell and to assure me that my sins were washed away. From the moment I arose from my knees, I have been a new creature in Christ Jesus. Wang-San Lao-Hu was dead, and instead I became a little lamb for Jesus. Yes, just a little lamb of the Lord Jesus!"

He repeated this as an expression of tender sweetness transfigured his countenance. "And ever since I have been telling men and women of His grace, His love, and His saving power."

An incense-bearer of the fragrance of Christ!

Oh, the love that sought me,

Oh, the blood that bought me,

Oh, the grace that brought me to the fold,

Wondrous grace that brought me to the fold.

LEE-BORN-OF-THE-SPIRIT

MIGHTY IN PRAYER

AND FAITH

The church in the Eighth Village was in an uproar. Every tongue was wagging at the defection from sound morals of Deacon Lee-Hope-to-get-Rich. The more tolerant souls were urging that a little less acrimony be directed toward him, since after all (it appeared that) he was more a victim than an instigator of the untoward circumstances which now engulfed him.

Deacon Lee was an itinerant peddler of books, the books being predominantly novels and folk-lore of none too good repute. Since becoming connected with the Hall of the Jesus doctrine, his way of life had not visibly altered to the outside world, and though he had been elevated to the exalted office of deacon by the election of his fellow-members, it was rather in deference to the fact that he was a man of persuasive eloquence than because of any outstanding spiritual qualities. In fact he was distinctly sub-par in the esteem of those who had in pretence or in truth embraced the name of Christ.

There had been, however, up to this time no outstanding charge against him. Even though she was childless, he had been faithful to his wife and had never made the slightest move to take an additional wife in the hopes of having children to carry on the family tradition. The latter course was both desirable and advisable according to the ancient code of his nation, and his heathen relatives had urged him to pursue it. But he had steadfastly eschewed it as being out of keeping with the customs of Jesus Hall.

It came to pass that one of Deacon Lee's brothers, having migrated to the city of Nanking, had prospered in business. In accordance with the traditions of clan loyalty, he cast around in his mind for some means of enhancing the power and increasing the numbers of the House of Lee.

He thought of the fact that his elder brother, Lee-Hope-to-get-Rich, had neither gotten rich nor produced sons, the latter failure being the more lamentable of the two. The difficulty had been further aggravated because his brother, having joined himself to the Jesus Hall of the foreign doctrine, had insisted on denying himself a second wife and the chance of posterity by reason of the rules and practices of that queer organization.

He decided to divorce him from such silly scruples by forcing his hand. He therefore purchased an eligible daughter from an impecunious father, paid her traveling expenses for the journey up the Grand Canal and across the country, and sent her on her way to the ancestral village.

Deacon Lee answered a knock on his door and found a strange damsel standing without. When he inquired what her business was, she informed him that she sought one Lee-Hope-to-get-Rich, saying that she had come from Nanking at the behest of his brother to become his wife! In token of which she produced documentary evidence, receipts, bills of lading, etc.

Imagine a pious churchman in such a predicament. To say that the deacon was flabbergasted would be to speak conservatively. His first amazement gave place to baffled fury. He was between Scylla and Charybdis. If he took her into his home, his reputation with his fellow communicants at the Jesus Hall would be damaged well-nigh beyond repair. If he turned her away to tell her story to all and sundry in the streets, the House of Lee would become a public laughingstock.

He chose the first as the least bitter of the two pills, received the unwelcome woman from the South into his house, and ordered that she be entertained as a guest.

Knowing that the news would fly on the wings of the wind, he hastened around to the Jesus Hall to explain how he had been victimized by his brother, an expert in the vicious ways of the South.

Such a juicy topic of conversation had not been forthcoming in years and was the occasion for the bedlam of gossip to which we referred at the outset of this history.

The war of words continued to rage over a period of weeks, during which time the deacon was striving feverishly to marry off his unwelcome guest to any eligible male in sight. To all such he dilated upon the charms, culture, and beauty of the fair one from the South, his main problem being to conceal his eagerness to be rid of her.

Negotiations were under way with several parties within the church and without, and the freshness of the event to Deacon Lee having worn off, the discussion had considerably abated. His obviously sincere attempts to marry her off, coupled with the kindlier counsels of the better-disposed, had gradually eased the tension and cooled the flames of criticism.

It seemed, however, that there was yet further chastisement in store for Mr. Lee. He had arrayed himself in his best gown on a bright Sunday morning to attend the house of worship. Two of his best friends had dropped by to accompany him to the morning service. As the three issued from the front door and out on to the threshing floor, Mr. Lee still hoping-to-get-rich observed that one branch of the locust tree, beside the threshing floor and in close juxtaposition to the large circular cesspool, was hanging limp and broken. He stopped and gave a grunt of displeasure as he mentally debated his most profitable course. If he left the branch in that condition, some neighbors might take advantage of his absence and relieve him of a piece of prospective firewood. On the other hand, to do anything in the way of servile work on the Sabbath would not commend his piety to the elders who were with him. That which the Chinese has in common with a Scotsman won the day. He asked his friends to wait a moment as he hastened back into the house and presently came out again with a small bench in his left hand and a saw in his right.

He placed the bench under the drooping branch, near the edge of the cesspool, stood upon it, and proceeded to saw. Perhaps you have already guessed it, but if not, here it is. In the midst of his effort he overbalanced himself on the rickety bench and, still grasping the saw, he plunged headlong into the unspeakable filth of the cesspool. His friends who witnessed the tragedy found it convenient to regard it as a divine visitation on the ubiquitous Mr. Lee and fled in terror, leaving him to extricate himself from his woeful plight.

They burst in upon the assembly gathered for worship and informed them of this further misfortune that had overtaken Mr. Lee. Pandemonium was again let loose. "Kai ying—Kai Ying!" "Just punishment, just punishment. We told you so," shouted those who had formerly been so quick to denounce Mr. Lee.

The humiliation of poor Mr. Lee was complete. For weeks after his interment in filth, he did not show his face at the Jesus Hall, even though in that time he had vindicated himself with respect to the woman from the South by contracting a marriage for her to a respected member of the church and community.

A proud, garrulous busybody had been buffeted into

docile humility by the kindly chastening of a loving God. Thus does our God move in mysterious ways to accomplish His purposes—to visit mercy on some and chastisement on others.

It was a quiet, unobtrusive Mr. Lee who resumed attendance at the Jesus Hall when we came to the Eighth Village to preach the Word of God. On about the fourth day of the meeting, we gave messages on the meaning of the Cross, the propitiatory death of Christ. We showed that the Cross is the condemnation of the world and the complete proof of the futility of human works. We showed that Christ suffered the essence of hell and separation from God, and only as we sinners recognize that only by His being made "afar off" from the Father can we be "made nigh;" only by His being "made sin" could we be "made righteous."

At the conclusion of the afternoon message, as we felt the Holy Spirit was gripping hearts in conviction, we gave an invitation for those to come forward who would truly receive of His grace and confess themselves dead, buried, and risen with Christ.

There was a fine response as numbers came forward, knelt down, and cried aloud to God for forgiveness of sin. One of the first was Mr. Lee. He wept and confessed himself to have been a hypocrite, covetous, a schemer, a busybody, proud, self-righteous; and he declared God's judgments on him to have been entirely just. He then gave a confession and testimony to the whole assembly, declaring that that day salvation had come to him for the first time.

From that hour Mr. Lee was truly a new creation in Christ Jesus. His change of heart took immediate effect on his conduct. He went home and got the remainder of his stock of books that he'd been selling and brought them to the church and placed them on the ground in the middle of the courtyard.

He invited the preachers and Christians who were assembled to inspect the books and whichever ones they thought unfitting for a Christian to sell or handle to throw into a pile on the side.

Several of the young preachers squatted beside the pile and glanced through each book. All the books, with the exception of some of the classics of Confucius and Mencius, which were regarded as innocent enough, were tossed on the discard pile.

But Mr. Lee did not falter. Before the whole group of spectators, he set fire to these books that represented practically the whole of his meager capital, and they were consumed in the flames.

"From this time on," he announced loudly, "I shall devote myself to selling the portions of God's Word and telling men of His saving grace."

This demonstration of abandoned sacrifice created a profound impression and silenced even his severest critics and accusers.

It was a few weeks later and we were preaching in another village in the same section of the country, about twenty miles from the Eighth Village. Facing the audience one morning, we saw the shining face of Mr. Lee-Hope-to-get-Rich, as he had previously been known.

After the service he came back to the little thatched hut that served as my apartment, in which porcelain wash bowls, running water, and electric lights were conspicuous for their absence.

"I want to give you my card," he began.

I assured him that I knew exactly who he was and did not need any identification.

"Oh, but you must have my new card! I have a new name. Formerly I was known as Lee-Hope-to-get-Rich. Now," he said, handing me his card with a flourish, "this is my name."

We glanced at the card and read the characters Lee-Ling-Sen, which means Lee-Born-of-the-Spirit.

"Nine years ago," he explained, "I was introduced to Christ. Not until the day you preached on the Cross of Christ was I really born of God. From henceforth I have no desire to get rich, so I have given up the old name; I am now a new creature—born of the Spirit of the Living God. From henceforth I live to tell others of Him."

Two years passed. The Lord led our steps into various parts of China, and we returned from time to time to our home in the lower Yangtze Valley. Upon returning home on one occasion, we found a great fat letter addressed in Chinese. Breaking the seal I found a sheaf of pages, neatly inscribed in Mandarin style. I wondered who could be my voluminous correspondent, so I turned immediately to the last page where, under the benediction "The peace of the Gospel unto thee," appeared in bold characters the name Lee-Born-of-the-Spirit.

"Aha!" we thought, "the erstwhile book salesman of the chequered career and the new name."

After the usual salutations, Mr. Lee went on to tell of his spiritual history since he had become Lee-Born-of-the-Spirit.

"I have preached the Word of God wherever I went as I have distributed and sold portions of Scripture. God has given me deep understanding of His Word, and I have become mighty in faith and prayer, so that the Lord has been glorified in me in the salvation of many souls and the healing of many bodies. All the people know that I can prevail in prayer to God.

"I will give a specific illustration, so that you may know that God's Word through you to me was not in vain. Last spring the drought in our section was very severe. The wheat sown in the fall had had no snowfall to blanket it during the winter, which was extremely dry. In the early spring no rains came to soften the ground. The villagers were busy invoking their gods, stretching the usual willow sprigs on strings across the streets. The village idol had even been brought out and carried around so that he could see the arid conditions. But still he did nothing about it.

"The people became alarmed as week after week passed and there was not a drop of rain. Famine was staring them in the face." (Where there is such a short interval between hand and mouth, the farmer's concern is everyone's concern.)

I read on as Mr. Lee told of a day when there was a knock upon his door. When he opened it, he found four village elders standing without.

"Come in gentlemen, and sit down."

As they crossed the court to his guest room, he shouted the command, *"Pao Ts'a*—Brew tea!" in response to which his wife came with a teapot and several cups. The beverage served on this occasion could be called tea only by courtesy. It was not the aromatic tea of the "Dragon Well," usually served in the homes of the wealthy, but the willow-leaf home brew in common use in the rural homes.

"What can I do for you today?" inquired Mr. Lee.

"We know, Mr. Lee-Born-of-the-Spirit, that you pray to a certain Jesus, and we are told that you receive remarkable answers to your prayers. We are requesting, therefore, that you shall pray to your Jesus to send rain upon this dry and thirsty land. You know we are all desperate as we contemplate the prospect of a famine."

"Oh," said our friend Lee, not without a touch of irony, "you gentlemen have found the *T'u ti Lao Yie* (the god of the fields) has not been able to help you out? Now you come around and ask me to pray my Jesus to send rain down on a lot of idolaters who do not believe in Him. I shall do nothing of the kind, so if that is all you have to say, you may take your departure."

"But Mr. Lee," they protested, "you will not refuse us so hastily. Is there anything we can do that will make you change your mind and supplicate your Jesus for us?" (thinking, of course, that a financial barter was in the offing). But this Lee-Born-of-the-Spirit proved to be not of the spiritual seed of Balaam, son of Beor.

"Yes," he said, "there are conditions, but they are not what you think. I demand no money and desire none, but you as heads of the village will be required to take down every idol or idolatrous symbol of any kind out of your homes and remove your ancestral tablets. All of these things must be brought out and publicly burned in the marketplace before I shall utter one prayer to my Jesus to relieve your drought."

The *Dong Sz* or village fathers were speechless at this. They had come prepared to accept a financial proposition, but such conditions as these were beyond their remotest thoughts. They looked blankly at one another till one suggested that he should give them time to think over his terms. To this he agreed.

Another week and the heavens remained as brass, the ground was cracking, and the sprigs of wheat long obscured by dust were beginning to turn yellow.

Again the four village fathers presented themselves at the home of Mr. Lee-Born-of-the-Spirit.

"Though your terms were unexpected and unusual, we have decided that we will meet them. We shall remove every Buddhist idol and every idolatrous symbol from our homes. We only beg of you that you will not require us to remove our ancestral tablets. We cannot offend the spirits of our forebears by removing them. If we did we would be guilty of breaking the basic law of filial piety. Nor do we consider this as idolatry."

"Do you not worship several times a year before these tablets of your ancestors?" inquired Brother Lee. "Can your ancestors who have died, and most of whom are in perdition, help you? Indeed it is right and proper for you to honor and respect your ancestors, but to worship them is idolatry, and I cannot pray to my Jesus for you while you are yet guilty of this sin. Unless you are willing to do away with your ancestral tablets, you may as well take your departure."

Sadly they went away, grumbling at the intolerance of these Jesus-worshippers. Another week of drought and in final desperation they returned to Mr. Lee and told him they were prepared to take down even their ancestral tablets if he would only pray for rain.

"Go, then, to your homes and remove all of these things to the open marketplace. I will presently come and inspect your homes and see that all is clear."

After a little delay, he made the rounds to the homes and inspected very carefully. Not a single idolatrous symbol could he find, and even the ancestral tablets had disappeared. He then went to the marketplace, where a large crowd was assembled. The four elders were in the center of the crowd with a pile of images, paintings, paper hangings and money, kitchen gods—Lares and Penates—and ancestral tablets.

Mr. Lee delivered a sermon to the assembled multitude on the one living and true God and the mediator between God and man, the Man, Christ Jesus. In the light of God's revelation, he declared the iniquity of idolatry and asserted the drought to be divinely sent as a punishment for their sin.

"This day, after we have burned these idols, we shall pray to Jehovah God in the name of His Son and there will be rain!"

He then proceeded to burn the pile of idols and fetishes, as grave predictions of impending disaster were whispered among the bystanders.

When the fire had abated, Mr. Lee ordered the elders to repair to his home for the season of prayer. He caused them to kneel down on the mud floor of his house, and he knelt beside them. For an hour and a quarter, Lee-Born-of-the-Spirit poured out his heart, citing God's power and His promises from Genesis to Revelation, pleading with Him to unbare His arm and vindicate Himself in the presence of a wicked and idolatrous people. There was no thought of glorifying himself. Even the physical needs of the people were not prominent in the supplications, but that the glory of God should be manifest.

Never had the elders of the village been subjected to

such an ordeal. At the end of the lengthy prayer, they issued forth and cast their eyes skyward. There was not a cloud in the sky. In an undertone they grumbled their doubt and incredulity.

Lee was standing in his doorway, watching them depart. Sensing their remarks, he shouted to them to go on home and eat their dinner. "And you will hardly finish eating before there is rain on the earth."

Each went to his own home and ate his bowl of steaming dry rice with an appetizer of bean sprouts and greens. Halfway through the repast and over the sound of rice being inhaled came the faintest sound of distant rumbling. The clacking of chop sticks ceased; there was even a diminuendo in chewing as one stared significantly at another.

Mr. Sun laid down his chop sticks and went out to scan the sky. Low on the horizon he spied some rain clouds. The rumbling came again, plainer than before.

"*Hao!*" he said and hurried into the house to report his discovery. "*T'ien fan*—Add rice," he commanded his wife as he extended his bowl. He devoured the remainder with added zest as from three points of the compass the clouds mounted higher and the sun was obscured.

Clumps of people were gathered in the open, watching the assembly of the rain clouds, until the most skeptical were forced to admit the imminent descent of the much-desired rain. Great streaks of lightning zig-zagged from the dome of heaven.

"*T'a shuoa dih, Lee shien-sen shuoa dih!*—He said it, Mr. Lee said it would come!"

A great gust of wind and then a mighty calm, then the large drops of rain fell singly and scattered, and then with increasing intensity until all had withdrawn to shelter. The torrent continued well-nigh unabated until the third day, till the elders of the village with wide oiled-paper umbrellas and hobnailed shoes picked their way through mud and water to the home of Lee-Born-of-the-Spirit.

"Mr. Lee, your Jesus has power indeed and has sent an abundance of rain. But if this continues, we shall have a flood. Will you not now supplicate your Jesus to cause it to cease?"

"Return to your homes. By eleven o'clock the sun will shine."

It was as he said. By eleven the sun shone brightly in a naked heaven.

Lee's letter concluded: "The crops were saved and in fact were better than usual and God the Father and God the Son were honored, and many opened their hearts to the gospel of His grace."

"Where is the God of Elijah?" you ask? Lee-Born-of-the-Spirit, mighty in prayer, demonstrated that He still lives and is the same.

Hu, the Elder

Looking for

the Blessed Hope

Mr. Hu-Resembling-Prosperity sat amidst regal splendor in the guest room of his spacious establishment in the Hu family village. He was the feudal lord of the town, the undisputed autocrat of all he surveyed, the possessor of extensive agricultural acreage in the surrounding country and the largest mansion in the center of the village with numerous courts and a hundred rooms. So august was his presence that none of the lesser lights in his family or among the rank and file villagers were permitted to sit down in his presence.

He was served his meals in solitary majesty. Before he sat down to his repast, he would look carefully at the appetizer in each saucer. If any dish looked to be poorly prepared or unworthy to appear on the table of his highness, he would verify his suspicions by lifting the saucer to his nose for a whiff and would then hurl the whole with its contents through the open door and into the courtyard. With all his irascibility and domineering qualities, the Elder Hu had a real fraternal interest in the welfare of his people and was fair and just in the administration of local affairs.

On the particular day of which we speak, as the Elder reposed in a semi-reclining wicker chair, a servant came in bearing a letter which he reported had been brought by special messenger from Elder Chu of the village of Yee-Hsu, forty li distant.

Mr. Chu was a lifelong friend of Mr. Hu, of corresponding position in his village. They also shared an interest in the writings of the sages, which they would discuss into the wee hours on their periodic visits to one another. The friendship was further cemented when Mr. Hu's eldest daughter was given in marriage to the first son of Mr. Chu.

Mr. Hu received the letter with a grunt, broke the seal with deliberation, and extracted a single thin sheet with vertical red lines at intervals of about half an inch, which were entirely disregarded in the inscription of the artistic grass characters of Mr. Chu. Real beauty and symmetry lie in that which to the unpracticed eye appears to be a careless hen scrawl.

The missive was brief but revolutionary in its import to Elder Hu. His eyes first ran easily over the characters. Then they began to blaze with wrath. The content of the letter was something like this:

Mr. Hu-Resembling-Prosperity, the Great One, the Worshipful One,

The small brother [designating the writer] has in the past been a student of the philosophies of the sages, a devotee of the three religions. Now, the small brother has found the true doctrine of the Mean, the mediator between God and Man, the Man Christ Jesus. If you care to discuss the matter, come and visit me when you have the opportunity.

The autumn's peace be unto thee,

The diminutive brother,

Chu Yuan-Shan

Rereading the epistle to assure himself that there was no mistake, Mr. Hu jumped to his feet in a rage, threw the letter down on the tile-paved floor, and stamped upon it with both feet.

"He has found the 'true doctrine of the Mean,' has he? Did not the philosopher Mencius enunciate the Doctrine of the Mean sufficiently well that he has to turn aside to this foreign Jesus?"

He was well-nigh speechless with anger that a master scholar of Chinese literature and philosophy should be guilty of such a horrible defection. He ignored the letter and sent the messenger back empty-handed as a deliberate rebuff to his old crony who had so seriously apostatized.

During the months that followed, the subject haunted him. He tried his best to account for this strange mental aberration on the part of his old friend, and he debated every angle of it until he was brain weary. He was torn between resentment at his friend's unaccountable departure from the precepts of the fathers and curiosity as to its cause.

Were Chu a mere yokel of the fields untaught in the four books and five classics, this talk of discovering the 'true doctrine of the Mean' could be attributed to ignorance, but Chu is a master of arts and can recite the classics by heart from beginning to end. Again, were he a pauperized scholar, he might be doing something to help himself by trying to reap financial gain by embracing the foreign doctrine, but Chu is a plutocrat, the owner of many fields.

Baffled in his attempt to explain the phenomenon, Hu saw the lunar year draw to a close. He now wished he could hear again from his friend Chu. He began to regret his refusal to send a reply to the short letter of a few months back. Since then, Chu had maintained an unbroken silence.

The New Year came on with its round of festivities, gambling, drinking, "worshipping the year." It was a time when convention demanded the Elder should receive and entertain with cakes and candy the endless stream of village swains in all stages of inebriation who would come in to pay their respects to him and bow before his ancestral tablets. He was bored to extinction at the very prospect of it and felt an urge to smash every precedent by going away and leaving it all.

The idea flowered on the first day of the big year, when he ordered his household servant to summon his wheelbarrow man. The servant's amazement at such a suggested profanation of the great day caused the domestic to partially forget the augustness of The Presence, and he muttered, "On the first day of the year?"

"Summon the wheelbarrow man," roared the great one, whereupon the servant beat a hasty retreat to carry out the mandate. Presently the wheelbarrow man stood before the master, resplendent in holiday attire, a blue percale external toga shiny with newness covering the old wadded garments beneath and a new satin hat surmounted by a bright red button set squarely on his head.

He bowed sedately, placing the ends of his sleeves together as he murmured the New Year salutation: *"Lao Hsien, Kong she, fah ts'ai re ee."* "May the venerable gentleman be felicitated with happiness, wealth, and health."

With a nod and a none-too-gracious grunt, Mr. Hu proceeded with the business in hand. "Prepare the wheelbarrow. I am going to Yee-Hsu."

Astounding as was such an order on such a day, he bowed and retired. The wheelbarrow was taken out of a locked room and trundled into the court. It was upholstered with a cotton comforter roped securely on one side of the high wheel in the center. The barrow-man unbuttoned his New Year garment and the wadded garments underneath, slipped his arms out of the four layers at one time and folded the whole carefully and placed it in the burlap catch-all suspended beneath the barrow, and informed the master that all was ready for departure.

The old gentleman presently issued forth with as many layers of clothing on as he could carry, high boots to cover feet and legs, and a massive hood covering his head, from which only his nose and mustache were visible. He sat on the upholstered side of the barrow, tucked one leg under, and allowed the other to dangle. The man who was to provide the power stood waiting, a woven strap with a loop in each end, over his stalwart shoulders. When the old gentleman was comfortably seated, he stooped over, slipped the loops over the ends of the shafts, and trundled Mr. Hu out of his gate and down the street of his village for a visit, the duration of which none knew, himself included. The townspeople exclaimed to themselves in muted undertones at this strangest of all acts of the old patriarch.

Four hours were required to cover the thirteen miles from the mud-fenced village of the Hu family to the town of Yee Hsu, and the short winter's day was drawing to a close as the iron rimmed wheel of the wheelbarrow rumbled noisily over the well-worn flagstone pavement of the street inside the gate, to break rudely upon the New Year stillness of a normally busy thoroughfare. Doors of stores boarded to the outside were inwardly the scenes of Bacchanalian festivities and gambling orgies.

A man at the side of the street, seated by a table on which there rested a Book, was the only human visible to the stranger on the wheelbarrow. The lone man was Elder Chu himself. He looked up at the sound of the approaching vehicle and immediately recognized the traveler in spite of his wraps. He hastened to meet him and in his joy at seeing his friend, forgot all decorum and threw his arms around Mr. Hu in a warm embrace as he cried, "I knew you would come, and I know you are going to be saved. I know you are going to be saved! You came out of your gate on the first day of the big year. I know you going to be saved."

"For shame!" sputtered Mr. Hu, thrusting him away, "for you to act in this undignified fashion and shouting all that jargon that 'you know I am to be saved.' And what mean you, the head of this village, to be sitting in the street behind a table with a book on it as though you were an ordinary fortune teller?"

"Come along in and have some hot tea and rice," said Chu, "and we shall discuss everything at our leisure."

Here began a visit of several weeks, during which the scholar Chu expounded enthusiastically to a stolid and truculent Hu a revelation of the grace of God in Christ. Visibly softened though yet unconvinced, it was midway through the second month before Elder Hu returned to the fenced village of Hu, laden with a Bible and several commentaries written by Faber, an early German missionary who had become a master scholar of Chinese. These he promised Chu to read carefully.

"The marvelous logic of the Book of Romans, under the

guidance of the scholar Faber, laid hold upon me," Mr. Hu told me in later years. "It was superb. Unanswerable. Unique! I fell down on my knees and confessed my sin and Christ my Savior and wrote a letter to my friend Chu saying, 'I too have now believed in the Christ of Calvary, the mediator between God and mankind.'"

Rarely, if ever, have we missionaries encountered such deep devotion to the oracles of God—to the person of Christ! Such a lofty concept of the undiluted grace of God. Such tender solicitude that others should be informed of it. The autocrat had abdicated; the ambassador of Christ had succeeded.

Now the humblest farm hand, with dust caking his clothes, would be invited to a seat of honor as the aging Elder Hu hobbled on crutches to pour tea for him, after which he would tell him of the grace of God in Christ.

Hu's wisdom as village father was enhanced after he came into fellowship with the Source of Wisdom. The rest of the country was scourged with bandits. The largest villages had been raided and looted and the leading citizens carried off for ransom, the local militia helpless to withstand the onslaught of the desperadoes.

But Elder Hu outmaneuvered them. He picked a brave and able man for Sergeant of Militia and commanded that the men should be carefully selected, well-paid, and adequately uniformed and equipped, and that the men should be constantly and carefully schooled in marksmanship. The courage, efficiency, and deadly aim of the militia detachment of the Hu village were so noised abroad that the town became a city of refuge for the terror-stricken burghers of other towns, till property values were at a high premium and there was considerable concentration of wealth within the walls. The town had never been attacked.

One day Mr. Hu received a message from the bandit chieftain who had scourged and bled the whole country. He wrote, "The country is a great circle like unto a nether mill stone and you are the hub at the center. We have done our will on all four sides and now we are coming after the hub. If you will pay us [two hundred thousand dollars] I will spare you; otherwise we shall attack and it will fare very much harder with you."

Deep consternation spread through the town of Hu. Several of the leaders came in to confer with Mr. Hu and tremblingly advised that the chieftain's demand be met.

"I shall do nothing of the kind," said Mr. Hu. "If we give him two hundred thousand dollars now, he will demand the same amount or more ten days later. Our sergeant here will set a watch on the tower and our men shall be kept in constant readiness on the walls, and I shall tarry each night in the bottom room of the tower praying to the Lord of Hosts for His care and protection."

Whereupon Mr. Hu sent word to the bandit chief that he would give him nothing. If he chose to attack he would find the men of Hu village prepared.

A few nights later an attack was attempted, but the volleys of lead from all parts of the wall were so disastrous to the bandits that they beat a hasty retreat and decided to confine their efforts to localities where the competition was less keen.

One week I was enjoying a wonderful visit in Hu's home, preaching to his people and discussing the things of God with him each night till the wee hours. Particularly did he love to speak of the hope of the near return of Christ. The next day he said, "I have something to show you."

I followed him as he called for his servant to get certain keys and then hobbled on his crutches through several circular gateways and through a series of courtyards. Presently he stopped before a two-leafed door and ordered the servant to unlock it. All that could be seen in the room when the doors were thrown open were two coffins. Of excellent workmanship they were and finished with the finest varnish, but coffins nevertheless.

For the sake of those who do not know, be it known that the Chinese of the better classes always prepare their coffins and their graveclothes long before their demise. They have no intention of being placed in just any kind of box or clad in just any sort of clothing for the body's long rest, so they superintend the construction of their own caskets and the tailoring of their own graveclothes.

After casually glancing at the two coffins, one for himself and the other for his wife, I asked him why he was taking such pains to show me the coffins, and assured him that I was not terribly interested in such things. He stamped his good foot with the least touch of irritation and commanded me to look well. I turned again and scanned the caskets and noticed something about them that I had previously overlooked.

At the bottom of each were four large characters carved into the wood and embossed with gold. The first four were *Wen sheng ts'u mo*—which literally means "Hear the sound and emerge from the grave." The other four read *Chu lai fu ch'ee,* which can be freely rendered, "At the Lord's coming I shall rise again."

Now I knew why he showed me the coffins. I bowed from the waist and congratulated the venerable gentleman on his sure hope of resurrection.

"That," he said, beaming, "will be my final testimony! When they bear me out in that box and the people along the street will say, 'Mr. Hu, the Jesus-believer is gone. But what mean those characters?' Then my own people are instructed to inform them all what *Wen sheng ts'u mo* means. They will say, 'Think not the Elder Hu is to be buried for all time. The characters mean that one day he will hear the voice of the Archangel and the trump of God, and he will come out of the grave and be raptured to heaven with a glorified body. God's Word declares it and it will be so."

So keen was the old gentleman on the truth of the Lord's coming that he insisted we must have a special afternoon meeting at the little mud-thatched church to set forth that momentous subject.

About an hour before the time for the service, the patriarch hobbled out of his gate on his crutches and moved down the street of his village to invite the villagers to the meeting.

He spied a fellow standing on the top rung of a ladder repairing the thatch on his roof. "Come down from there!" commanded Mr. Hu, "don't you know the pastor is going to preach on the coming of Christ? Get your family and hurry over to the church." Immediately he began to back down the ladder.

A moment later Hu addressed a man behind a store counter. "Where's your daughter?" inquired Mr. Hu.

"In the back yard," replied the proprietor.

"Call her to come and wait on the trade, and you and your wife and son come over to the church to hear the pastor preach on the return of Christ."

"Hao, hao—ma sang chiu lai," that is, "Good! I will be there with the speed of a horseman."

Further down the road in an open space, a yokel stood holding a cow by a line fastened to a ring in her nose, while she contentedly ate her hay.

"Hitch that thing!" yelled Mr. Hu, "why should you stand there like a wooden man when the pastor is preaching on the coming of Christ? Make no delay in coming to the church."

Needless to say, the little church was jammed beyond

capacity, and the people stood in the courtyard. For an hour and a half, the old gentleman sat erect on a backless bench six inches wide and listened with rapt interest to the message of the near advent of Christ in light of fulfilled prophecy.

The meeting over, we felt the old gentleman should get back to his home as quickly as possible. We had a Harley-Davidson motorcycle with side-car in the courtyard and persuaded him to entrust himself to that outrageously noisy contraption. We packed him in the side-car—crutches and all. As I threw my leg over to kick over the starter, Mr. Hu did not appear entirely happy, and when the engine fired with a series of explosions, the old man's face was a study in fear. We whirled out of the courtyard and onto the undulating dirt road. The steel rimmed wheels of countless ox carts had transformed the road into little better than a series of camel humps. The jerky motion of cycle and sidecar even at the speed of 20 mph was reminiscent of the sensation one experiences on a carnival thriller. Accustomed to the placid progress of a wheelbarrow, Mr. Hu felt himself to be traveling at blinding speed, at least half of which was up and down. He was almost convinced that the rapture was already begun.

We circled the village and entered at his south gate, finally drawing up in front of his mansion. We extricated him from the side-car and helped him through the courtyards into his spacious sanctum.

One would think that such a harrowing experience

would have banished from the old man's mind the message of the afternoon. But he had no more than deposited himself in the semi-reclining wicker chair before he straightened up and whisked back each sleeve preparatory to issuing a manifesto.

"It will not be long!" he said. "You younger men will live to see it. Unless He comes within the next year or so, they will put me in that casket out there. But even I will not have to sleep very soundly. I will only nod a little while before the trumpet sounds."

We shall never forget the triumphant radiance of his countenance, an incense bearer of the Son of God.

"Even so, come, Lord Jesus!" (Revelation 22:20).

ERNEST AND FAITH

A MODERN AQUILA AND

PRISCILLA

The Yins are a well connected and distinguished family, with their origins in the Province of Hunan. Into this family, over half a century ago, was born a son who later received the school name Ren-Sien, which might be freely rendered, "Duty First."

Young Ren-Sien was educated in his early years and, as befitted his position in the old style classical manner, drilled in the writings of the sages. Later he was sent down the river to the great educational center of Nanking, where he was initiated into some of the mysteries of Western learning and made contacts with organized Christianity. Here he assumed the Christian name of Ernest.

At some point, Ernest made a profession of faith and was received into the Presbyterian Church of Nanking. He is always at pains now, though, to make clear that this was only a profession; that is, it was not a genuine faith of the heart and was unaccompanied by the experience of regeneration.

Returning to his home, he was married at an early age and soon embarked upon a commercial career. Of this first union there were four children born—two girls and two boys, but after bearing Ernest these children, his young wife died.

Deeply grieved, Ernest sought a change of scenery. He determined to pursue further education, so committing his children to the care of his near relatives, he left the shores of China, sailed for the United States, and matriculated into Harvard University at Cambridge.

Four years later, he graduated, receiving his Bachelor's degree. After traveling back and forth between China and the U.S. for two years, he married a charming Chinese woman named Miss Sü-Yuin Ding, who had also been educated in America. She'd completed her undergraduate work at Mount Holyoke and then engaged in graduate zoology studies in Columbia.

Upon her return to China, Miss Ding became connected with the work of the Y.W.C.A., located in Shanghai. Here she was a colleague of Miss May-Ling Soong, better known in later years as Madame Chiang Kai-Shek.

Miss Ding was the daughter of the well-beloved pastor Ding Li Mei, one of the mightiest witnesses God has ever raised up in China, who even in his later years of failing health focused on the ministry of intercession. This dear man told me of the pangs of soul that he'd suffered when he discovered the destructive effects of Sü-Yuin Ding's American education upon the faith instilled in her since youth. He told me of a beautiful Bible he had given to the couple on the occasion of Sü-Yuin's marriage to Ernest Yin, and how disappointed he was several years later to learn that it lay still untouched in the bottom of a trunk.

After their marriage, Ernest and Sü-Yuin took up residence in the city of Tsinanfu, where Ernest held an excellent government position as Director of the Tax Bureau on Wines, Spirits, and Tobacco. They plunged into the whirl of society dinner parties, theater, mah-jong parties, and dances. They differed in no essential particular from the activities of the godless in any land at any time.

As the four siblings by the previous marriage were beginning to grow up and attend high school and college, another son was born to Ernest and Sü-Yuin and given the name David. Lena, the eldest daughter, attended Ginling College at Nanking. A few years later I encountered her and she related this testimony:

"I'd always had a spiritual mind and desired to know the things of God. When I was just a young girl in McTier's school in Shanghai, I would walk around the campus at night and look up at the stars and think, 'Surely the Creator of the heavens must have some purpose in us who are His creatures,' and yet, though it was a mission school, no one ever told me of the way of salvation. When I later attended Ginling College it was just the same. I still wondered but was not told of Christ the Savior and sin-bearer, the coming King. Then someone gave me a Bible and urged me to read the Gospel of John. It was in the reading of this Gospel and without human assistance or leading that I received Christ as my Savior.

"I had been rejoicing in salvation some months when I returned to my parents in Tsinan for a holiday. By this time we had another little brother by our stepmother. They had called him David, and he was the apple of our parents' eyes. I found that little David loved the Bible stories I told him and the gospel choruses I taught him to sing.

"My parents were tolerant toward me, but after some days they took me to task for not going out with the young set with whom I should normally have associated. I assured them that since I was a Christian I had no desire whatever to associate with that worldly group and greatly preferred to remain at home. I told them that I enjoyed the company of little David.

"They then upbraided me, not too unkindly, for my fanaticism in adhering to a set of outworn dogmas and thus threatening to spoil my life. My father went on to assure me that he and my mother had once thought there was something to all that, but after going to America and sitting at the feet of the great professors in the universities, they had been convinced that the Bible was merely Hebrew folklore, filled with errors and superstition, of no value to the intellectual people of the modern age.

"Yes indeed," said my mother, "I, being the daughter of Pastor Ding Li-Mei, was nurtured in the doctrines of Christianity but have been thoroughly disillusioned in the course of my education. It is not good enough, Lena, to waste your life on."

"My dear parents," I replied. "I highly regard your conclusions in most things, but I must say that if all the university professors in America unite to declare that the Bible is untrue, it cannot alter the fact that Jesus Christ lives in me and I am saved by faith in Him and His blood shed for me on the cross. And, my dear parents, Christ is very much grieved with you two, because having been taught of Him, you have cast it aside and have turned back to the world and its pleasures. Until I came home, little David had not been taught anything about the Lord Jesus, but now he loves to pray and sing gospel choruses. You both love little David very much, so sometimes I wonder if the Good Shepherd is not going to be compelled some day to take His little lamb back to the Father's House in order that the sheep may return to His path."

The meaning of the last statement was too obvious to be missed. It was a bold thrust but uttered with such quiet earnestness and respect that no offense could be taken. The conversation was thereby terminated.

A week later, Lena returned to her studies in Nanking and the other three siblings were scattered to diverse places. One afternoon, Mother was in the parlor playing the piano.

Little David was playing in the room. Occupied with her music, Mother failed to observe David slip out of the room. Presently she turned to speak to him, and seeing that he was gone, she went out into the hallway. Not finding him there, she called all the servants and asked if they knew where the little chap was. All denied having seen him, but joined in the search for the beloved son all over the house and spacious grounds.

An hour later they found him. The house was surrounded by a deep ditch full of water, somewhat similar to a moat surrounding a medieval castle. It was on the surface of this moat that the body of little David was found floating, face down. The Good Shepherd had come and taken the little lamb back to the Father's House.

The despair and sorrow in that home was overwhelming. A telegram was sent to Ernest Yin, who was in Tsingtao on business, and to each of the children to return immediately. The older siblings found Ernest and Sü-Yuin kneeling by the coffin, weeping pitifully. But in the depth of their sorrow, the Lord sent a beloved and godly physician to minister to them the Words of Life. He urged them then and there to turn from the things of the world and receive Christ as Savior and Lord. The Spirit of God moved in their hearts and drew them to the foot of Calvary.

Then and there these two children of Adam the First, by faith became the spiritual children of Adam the Last, and two errant sheep came back to the Father's Way.

As they mingled tears of repentance with tears of sorrow, the Savior gave them balm for their sorrow, the oil of joy for their mourning, and the garment of praise for the spirit of heaviness. They returned from the cemetery to devote themselves wholeheartedly to the Word of God and the testimony of Jesus Christ. So enthusiastic was Ernest's testimony to his subordinates in the Tax Bureau that they could only account for it by declaring that grief over the death of his son had deranged his mind.

Ernest and Sü-Yuin witnessed just as actively now in the society circles in which they moved. The transformation was immense and complete. For singleness of heart and zeal for Christ and His truth, few could equal this couple.

Less than two years after his conversion, Ernest Yin was transferred to Kaifeng, the capital of Honan, to a position in the provincial tax bureau of that province. By this time they had another little son, whom they called John. In Kaifeng the testimony of this flaming pair was more vigorous than before, and it was here that we made our acquaintance with them. I was called to Kaifeng for special meetings, and Ernest Yin would assemble his office force at dawn so as to dismiss them to attend the mid-morning service at the church.

At this time, James Tao-Yung, the eldest son of Ernest, was at home for the first time since his parents' conversion. This cultured, well-groomed young collegian did not know what to make of it. When I spoke to him of my hope and expectation that he also would be saved, he loosened up and blurted, "I don't know what to make of this family of mine!

When I left home this was a normal Chinese household. Now I come home, and at breakfast my father starts in on me: 'Tao Yung, you need salvation, you must believe on the Lord Jesus Christ and be saved.' Then my mother takes it up: 'Tao-Yung, you must be born again or you will never see the kingdom of God.' Then my sister, Lena, chimes in: 'Tao-Yung, we have all been saved and are going to Glory, but unless you believe in the Lord Jesus and be saved, you won't be with us.' And so it is, morning, noon, and night; breakfast, dinner, and supper, until I feel convinced that they have either gone mad or I have. I am perfectly willing to be saved, but I do not yet understand it all."

He came to the meetings regularly, and after one nightly meeting this fine young man came to me and said that his mind had been enlightened and his heart touched.

"Now," he said, "I am saved." He asked me to pray with him, and after I had committed him to Christ, he uttered a prayer of faith and thanksgiving.

And thus was each one in the Yin family added to God's family.

LENA AND JONATHAN

WHOM GOD HAS JOINED TOGETHER

On the same visit to Kaifeng that James became a Christian, his sister Lena asked to speak to me privately. When we were alone, she said, "I want to tell you of my temptation."

I have had enough experience to know that when a lovely young girl speaks of her temptation, it is very likely to wear trousers, and so it proved in this case.

She told me of an interrupted romance. When still a student in Ginling College at Nanking, she had become acquainted with a young student at the university.

"He is a very nice young man, you know," she said, "and a model of good character and behavior. He is so moral and upright that he feels he needs no Savior."

In reply to her witness, he would persist in saying, "I have no need to be a Christian. What is the use of it? I am already a better man than those who claim to be Christians."

So, though he would never attend Christian meetings, he

would kindly escort her to the door and would return later to pick her up afterward.

There are parts of Nanking within the city walls that are wide open spaces, where there are undulating hills, groves, gardens, and fields. One would seem to be in the country rather than in one of the greatest, most populous capitals in the world. It was while strolling along a road through just such a rustic scene that handsome Mr. Chang stopped and point blank asked the charming Miss Yin to marry him.

Miss Yin replied, "There is one serious objection to it. I am going to heaven and you are on your way to hell. How can two people who are traveling in opposite directions get married?"

With this reply all negotiations tending to matrimony broke down.

During the six years since, they had remained friends and had corresponded regularly though unromantically. And both had remained single.

"I have told you all this," Lena went on, "because I am interested in his salvation, and I'd like you to be on the lookout for him when you go to Nanking next week. I shall write to him to go hear you and greet you after the meeting."

I assured her that I would not forget.

As I headed toward Nanking after meetings in Kaifeng, I was accompanied on the train by Ernest Yin, who was seeking to round up his son Arthur and daughter Grace to also attend the meetings in Nanking. On the journey, Ernest spoke excitedly of his plans for the advancement of the work of the Lord in his region.

When the Nanking meetings opened, I noticed an excellently dressed young man in the audience at the first afternoon meeting. Afterwards he came up and introduced himself as Arthur Yin. He said his father had sent him up from Shanghai and he wished to "report himself present." Because of a university lab period, Grace would not be able to attend until the evening meeting.

At the evening meeting, I saw a young woman with Arthur I assumed to be Grace, and there was also a handsome young Chinese who sat on the front row dressed fastidiously in native costume and conducting himself with admirable attention and dignity.

After the service, this young man stood waiting to speak to me.

That, I thought, has to be Lena's boyfriend. And so it proved to be. He presented himself with a courteous bow and thrust his hand into his robe to withdraw a letter.

"You may save yourself the trouble of that letter of identification," I said. "You are Mr. En-pu Chang, the friend of Miss Lena Yin of Kaifeng. I am happy to meet you and glad to take this opportunity of introducing you to Mr. Arthur and Miss Grace Yin, a brother and sister of Lena."

They greeted one another with due decorum and, as they conversed, became fast friends. I am thrilled to report that before the series of meetings were over, all three came unreservedly to Christ and confessed Him as Lord and Savior.

Young Chang came to see me in the room where I stayed and gave his testimony. "I have been very self-righteous and have felt no sense of sin or need of a Savior. I was comparing myself with my fellowman. But the night you gave the message on the holiness of God as revealed to Isaiah, the Spirit of God showed me my awful sin and hypocrisy, and I immediately received Christ as Savior and Lord."

As Chang wrote out a long profession of faith to be delivered to the Yin family, I warned him lest he permit any natural affection for Lena to influence the all-important question of his relationship to Christ. He replied with some spirit that for six years he had never stooped to any pretense along that line and that he would not do so now.

Six months later I had the pleasure of joining the hands of Lena Yin and En-pu Chang in the holy bonds of matrimony. At that time he asked me to give him a Bible or "Christian" name.

"Do you really love the Savior, the Lord Jesus Christ?" I asked him.

"I do indeed!" he replied.

"David was like Christ in many ways and Jonathan, son of Saul, loved him as his own soul. I therefore dub thee Jonathan."

Since that day, En-pu has loved his Christian friends and others as Jonathan loved David. And he and Lena have been a beautiful and steadfast couple in the testimony of the Lord for many years.

ARTHUR AND GRACE

PRESENTED AT

THE KING'S COURT

During the six months in which the beautiful romance of Lena and Jonathan budded and blossomed into marriage, Arthur Yin, employed in a newly established bank in Shanghai, was receiving his baptism of fire as a soldier of Jesus Christ. This distinguished young graduate of Tsing Hua University was thrown into the midst of a whirlpool of iniquity in what is called the Paris of the Orient. On the occasion of a few visits I made to Shanghai in 1935, he sought me out in his free time and stayed with me in my room at the Missionary Home.

He sighed for a place of quiet in which to pray and read his Bible.

"My rooming house," he said, "is in the midst of a nest of gambling dens, brothels, theaters, and dance halls, and I long for a quiet room where I can go that is out of earshot of all this unholy clamor to read and pray."

I suggested to him a room near his banking establishment that was set aside for prayer.

Though we focused primarily on the Scriptures, our conversation ranged from economics to current events, from the various Chinese dialects to an analysis of Bill Tilden's tennis stroke. The fellowship was delightful and I rejoiced to see him grow in spiritual knowledge and understanding.

At Easter, Arthur and Jonathan traveled to the Chinkiang church where I was ministering to publicly confess Christ and to receive baptism. One could search the world over for two more cultured, courteous, charming young men than this pair, scions of the best families of old China, trophies of the grace of Christ.

Grace continued to pursue her studies in the University of Nanking, but with a new hope and joy. And when the warm days of summer came, the whole Yin family came to our home atop a lovely hill to celebrate the wedding of Lena and Jonathan. It was a memorable occasion with many friends present from China and the West.

The ceremony was planned to take place on the green lawn under some trees, but dark threatening clouds caused a last minute shift to the parlor. Though the rain poured, nothing could dampen the happiness of the occasion, and we rejoiced in all that the Lord had done.

As we look back on that felicitous occasion, it would seem that those thunderheads were the harbingers of sorrow that was to come shortly over that particular company. And on a more comprehensive scale they foreshadowed the war clouds that were to arrive a brief two years later.

Those were halycon days in Old Cathay, such as we do not expect to see again in this age. Not for a millennium had China enjoyed the tranquility that characterized the years from 1932 to 1937, with Chiang Kai-Shek at the helm.

The month of June was drawing to a close, and it was time for me to commence north to Peitaiho, a lovely seaside resort near where the Great Wall meets the Sea. Here, Summer Bible Conferences were held each year.

As I passed Nanking, I paid a brief visit to our newlyweds, Lena and Jonathan, in their home. When I left, they accompanied me to the railway station, for they were also to meet Lena's father, who was coming from Shanghai that very day.

When Ernest stepped off the train, he greeted us with characteristic warmth. His face shining, he informed me that he had arranged a vacation for Arthur from his bank so he could go north to attend the Peitaiho Conference and that Grace would join him in Nanking. Ernest added that he'd wanted them to travel with me that evening but they couldn't get away soon enough. Later I thought of how differently things might have turned out had they been with me instead of delaying a day.

The other brother, James, who had been converted in Kaifeng, was going to serve as secretary at the Conference.

He met me on the station platform when I arrived that Saturday afternoon. When I told him that his brother and sister would be along the next day he was delighted.

The next day was the date set by the Nanking Ministry of Railways to run the first train through from Peking to Mukden since the occupation of Manchuria by the Japanese in 1931. During that interval, there were two trains running, one from Peking to the Great Wall and one from outside the Wall to Mukden. Incensed by Japan's grab for Manchuria, the Chinese Nationalists felt that to fail to run a through train was for China, in effect, to formally recognize Japanese sovereignty in Manchuria. The Iron and Blood Society, a red-hot group of Nationalists, made several drastic threats regarding what they would do if the train were run through. The railway authorities ignored these threats and carried on with their plans.

It was this train that Arthur and Grace boarded at Tientsin when they transferred from the southern train. They usually rode in the first or second class compartments, but that day they went into the third class car.

The train was about sixty miles out of Tientsin when it became apparent that the warnings of the Iron and Blood Society were not empty threats. A time bomb had been placed in each of the first, second, and third class cars. Only the one in the third class car detonated, and it exploded almost directly under Arthur and Grace's seat.

The whole side of the car was blown out and quite a

number were killed or wounded. Arthur and Grace did not escape. A piece of shrapnel entered Arthur's throat just below the jaw, passed right up through his brain and shot through the top of his head. He never knew what hit him and never regained consciousness. Grace was horribly mangled. Her Manchurian gown was completely blown off, her skull crushed in, four fingers of one hand shot off, the calf and thigh of one leg ripped open, and the other foot split in half, hanging to her ankle by a thread. Still she was fully conscious.

The sun glared down on victims as they were laid out on a station platform, but Grace did not feel the searing heat. A master-sergeant of the United States Infantry Medical Corps was on the train and he knelt beside her to see if he could help.

She thanked him for his kindness and said, "I am going to die and go to be with the Lord Jesus Christ. I think you would do better to help the others. I would be glad if you can find my brother and see what can be done for him."

The master-sergeant later made a statement to the Press that though he'd served more than 1,200 wounded in the World War, he had never seen such a demonstration of courage as was shown by that Chinese girl.

"This girl," he added, "was really a Christian!"

A missionary also knelt beside Grace and took her name and the name of her brother. She told him they had been headed to the Conference of Christ being held at Peitaiho, but said she knew no one there except

Mr. Graham and her other brother.

Perhaps the girl realized then that she was going to meet Christ in a far greater and more real sense than she could have possibly done at Peitaiho. She suddenly grew quiet, and minutes later the spirit left the body and she fled to Christ's presence.

The news relayed to James and me was only that Grace and Arthur had been injured. James took the first train to the scene of the tragedy. He found the torn body of Grace already placed in a rude coffin and was told that James had been taken to a Tientsin hospital. He ordered Grace's coffin transported to Tientsin and hurried on to the hospital. All he found was his brother's corpse. Arthur had died on the trip to the hospital. James' grief was great, for no two brothers were ever more devoted to each other.

He committed the two corpses to a mortician and wired his father to come. Then he wrote a letter to me—one of the most beautiful I have ever received. In it he told how, even in death, the peace of God was written on those two faces. He also rejoiced that they were saved and had gone to be with the Lord. At the close of his letter, he asked if I would come the following Sunday to perform the funeral service. This I arranged to do.

Ernest Yin had arrived before me and came to meet me in the early morning, greeting me with affection and with that quiet sobriety that has always characterized him. He was no whit different from the man who had come to see his other daughter married at my home five weeks before.

He gripped my hand, looked heavenward, and said with a radiant smile, "I have no complaint to make, my Tao-Koa (Arthur) and Teh-Huei (Grace) are now in the presence of the Savior. I am filled with joy to know that they both received Him that day in Nanking." Ernest was never occupied with his own sorrow, but spent his time testifying of the saving power of Christ to the many guests who came.

The tragic event in which two shining young people of one of the best-connected and most widely-acquainted families in all China met sudden death received wide publicity, and the little chapel at the Race Course Road Cemetery in Tientsin was packed on that torrid Sunday afternoon.

An excellent opportunity was afforded me to bring the claim and privilege of the Gospel home to many who knew nothing of it. The message was drawn from 2 Corinthians 5:1 (KJV), "For we know that if our earthly house of this tabernacle were dissolved, we have a building of God, an house not made with hands, eternal in the heavens."

It was evident then and later that in what seems to humans the untimely death of two young people, the challenge to others for the immediate acceptance of Christ as Savior and Lord was tremendous and, in the wisdom of God, was permitted for this purpose.

Through this heartbreaking trial, the character and testimony of Ernest Yin emerged finer and stronger than ever.

"*Precious in the sight of the Lord is the death of his saints*" (Psalm 116:15, KJV).

THE KEEPER OF THE TREASURY

AND THE GOVERNOR

A few brief months after the passing of his son and daughter, I received a letter from Ernest Yin.

After the usual greetings, he wrote, "The Lord Jesus Christ has promoted me to be Commissioner of Finance for the Province of Honan. I shall accept this higher position for the glory of Him who gave me life."

As Tax Bureau Director, he wrote that he had turned in four times more revenues to the central government in Nanking than did his predecessor, so when the highest finance position in the province became vacant, he was immediately elevated to it. This placed him in a commanding position, with only the Governor his superior.

When he assumed the office of Finance Commissioner in September, the provincial treasury was $2,000,000 in the red. At the end of the fiscal year—June 30th of the next year—

it was $700,000 in the black. For the honesty and efficiency of his administration, Ernest was cited on the front page of the *Shun Pao,* one of Shanghai's great daily newspapers, in a conspicuous square of heavy black type.

Ernest concluded his letter with a request that I come and speak to a company of people whom he would invite into his home to hear the Word of God. This was what he had done before on a smaller scale, but his higher position made it possible for him to invite all of the official class and the intelligentsia. Though his invitation was in no sense intended as a mandate, it was not considered good form in those circles to ignore such invitations.

I was not able to go until late the following spring, but when I did, the Lord honored His Word and the zeal and devotion of Commissioner Yin. Men and women of the highly educated, elite class and Chinese students from the West heard the Word and received it. A commissioner in the Governor's cabinet and his wife were beautifully converted. The president of the provincial bank, as well as the agent for Ford Automobile in three provinces and their wives were all saved.

Ernest Yin was thrilled at this movement of the Spirit of God, but as he paced the floor of his home, I knew he was planning an offensive on another front.

Presently he stopped and said, "The governor! The governor! He has not been presented directly with the Gospel. I am not in a position to invite him to these nightly meetings, but we will invite him to a dinner party and give him the Gospel."

Never an enemy of good victuals, I accepted the challenge. The governor also accepted the invitation.

Excellently attired in the conventional long satin toga with the short sleeveless black vest, the swarthy, soldier-scholar appointed as head man by Generalissimo Chiang Kai-Shek presented himself at the home of Commissioner Yin at the appointed hour.

A scholar of the old school of China and a soldier of the new school, Governor Shang Cheng was bronzed with the suns of campaigns and training periods in the field. He had attained the rank of General before being assigned to a post of civil administration.

He knew a smattering of English and had had some contacts with Western diplomats in Peking while governor of the Province of Hopei in which the city of Peking is located. The Governor was the soul of genial courtesy during the course of the delightful feast provided by our host, and we engaged in casual conversation.

After dinner, we adjourned from the table to "sit widely." As Governor Shang sank comfortably into an upholstered chair, I spied a beautiful new copy of the Scriptures lying on the table. Lifting it from the table, I inquired if his Excellency had ever read it.

He scanned it carefully and said, "Ah! this is the 'Sheng Ching'—the Sacred Classic, is it not?" Then, in answer to my question, he said, "No, not much," which is polite way of saying never.

I opened it at random and my eyes fell on the beloved 53rd chapter of Isaiah. As I pointed with my finger down the columns, his eyes followed the reading of the characters. The words flowed in the matchless biblical Mandarin:

"Surely he has borne our griefs and carried our sorrows, yet we did esteem him stricken, smitten of God, and afflicted. But he was wounded for our transgressions, he was bruised for our iniquities, the chastisement for our peace was upon him and with his stripes we are healed.

"All we like sheep have gone astray, we have turned, every one, to his own way, and the Lord has laid upon him the iniquity of us all."

Here he stopped me for a moment and said, "What means all this, and to whom does it refer?"

"To the Lord Jesus, who is the sin-bearer of all who believe in Him, who took our punishment on the cross."

"Who wrote it?" he asked.

"A man by the name of Isaiah." I pointed to the book title in the margin.

"When did he write it?"

"About seven hundred years before Jesus Christ was born and about a century and a half before Confucius lived."

The Governor appeared perplexed. "Did I understand you to say that this Ee-Sai-Yah [Isaiah] wrote all these things about the death of Jesus Christ seven hundred years before Jesus Christ was born?"

"That is quite correct, Sir."

"Well, how could the man Ee-Sai-Yah know anything about it?"

"Because the Spirit of the Living God, who knows the end from the beginning, revealed these mysteries to him long before they came to pass."

"Seven hundred years before," mused this gentleman of Old Cathay.

The wonder of divine foreknowledge communicated to fallible men by the Holy Spirit gripped his imagination.

Presently he rose hastily from his seat as if to forcibly interrupt his meditations and announced that the pressure of official business demanded his presence at provincial headquarters. He bowed around the circle to guests and hosts, expressing his gratefulness. Then he turned to me, bowed to the waist, and extended his hand Western-fashion.

"I have a request to make of you. Could you come to my small place tomorrow and instruct me further in this wonderful matter foretold seven hundred years before? And Commissioner Yin [turning to our gracious host], could you accompany the pastor to my place, say at 10:00 a.m. tomorrow morning?"

We both assured him that we would be there at the time appointed.

With a nod and smile to all, he quickly made his exit. His personal bodyguard escorted him to his car, and he was whisked away to his offices.

The next morning at five minutes before ten, Ernest Yin and I were ushered into the parlors of the Governor's Mansion and served tea. On the tap of ten, the Governor appeared, this time attired in a close-fitting military suit of gray gabardine.

He welcomed us cordially, inquired as to whether we had been served tea, and then drew up a chair close to mine and said, "Tell me more of the matter of which you were speaking yesterday, of which the man spoke seven hundred years before it occurred."

Unhurriedly I explained the purposes of God through the ages and told of the Lamb, the sacrifice for sin, slain in the counsels of God before the foundations of the world, and of His sure return again to reign. The issue was made ever so personal, as well as the necessity of individual recognition of one's own sinful and lost estate before God.

He listened with intense and unflagging interest and then said, "Then what shall I do about it?"

"Kneel right here with me, and acknowledge Christ as Lord and Savior. Are you willing to do so?"

"Certainly, I am. Indeed, I must!"

Down on the beautiful Tientsin rug we knelt, and I first uttered a prayer and then led the Governor in a prayer of acceptance of and committal to Christ. He spoke the words as sincerely and earnestly as a child, and I feel sure that at that moment he became a child of God. No one who knows his Bible can escape the similarity of this experience to that of Philip and the Ethiopian eunuch.

Governor Shang never missed another evening meeting at the home of Commissioner Yin while I was there, and at the last invited us all to a dinner at his home where only the things of God were discussed.

As I journeyed to the northern cities of Tientsin and Peking to preach, he wired to friends in Tientsin to greet and entertain me, and wrote his wife, who was residing at their fine home in Peking, to come and hear the Word of God, a thing which she was careful to do.

The Governor wrote me a letter in halting English but with unmistakable sincerity in which he said he was thankful to God for bringing me to Kaifeng to "lead him into the way of truth and life."

In the calamitous war foisted upon China by Japan a year later, General Shang Cheng was one of the commanders of the Chinese army that made such a long and noble stand at Suchowfu. When the armies retreated inland he was in command of the divisions in the southern Province of Kiangsi. From Christian sources there, I heard of his continued testimony to the saving power of Christ and of his promotion to be a marshal in command of forty-two divisions of the Chinese armies.

In the midst of the stress and strain of war, the Lord

continued to make Ernest Yin and his wife shining lights for Himself. Transferred from Honan in hopes that he would revolutionize the finances of his native Hunan, he was offered the governorship of that province, but he refused to accept the offer. He did accept the portfolio of Finance Commissioner. Later, he was transferred to Chung-king, the Western capital of General Chiang, where he was right hand men to Dr. H.H. Kung, Finance Minister and brother-in-law to Generalissimo Chiang.

"He that believeth in me, from his innermost being shall flow rivers of living waters" (John 7:38).

A Scientist Meets the God

of Science

While preaching in Wuchang, one of the twin cities of central China, I noticed a well-dressed man seated in the rear of the church, looking rather bored. He had the pew to himself, so he put his foot up on the bench, braced his back in the corner of the pew, and prepared himself for a comfortable nap.

Presently I began to read Matthew, chapter 24, from the Mandarin Bible. The man in the rear of the hall began to prick up his ears just a wee bit and to evince some interest that the foreigner could read the Mandarin with a rather unusual degree of facility. Having read a portion of the great Olivet discourse containing the signs of the end of the age, I proceeded to give a message on the signs of the second advent of Christ, citing recent world conditions and international relationships, the general breakdown of morals, the departure from revealed truth, as fulfillments of the sign. The man on the back pew was unable to continue his nap. In spite of himself, he straightened his back, put both feet on the floor, and then leaned over on the pew in front with arms folded and chin on the back of his hands. His eyes burned into me as I set forth the truth of the near return of the Son of God.

After the service was over, he came down to the front to speak to me. Rarely have I seen such agitation. Sputtering in alternate English and Chinese, he began to shout, "It is true. It is true. Every word you say is true. I never knew these things were revealed in the Bible. May I go with you to your house and talk with you further concerning these matters?"

As we strolled to the house, I learned that he was the dean of the Science Department of a great university there in Wuchang and possessed a doctorate in philosophy from one of our American universities. We had a long and earnest conversation, and my friend, Dr. Cheng, really met the Lord Jesus. A fire was kindled within him the like of which I have never encountered before in a spiritual babe.

At the next few meetings he attended, he kept his Bible open and listened with avid interest. On Saturday evening, he told me about a certain friend, a Dr. Chow, whom he had brought in as a professor of mathematics in his department. His friend was in Shanghai in a hospital, and he felt he may die shortly from a serious kidney malady. As he told me about it, he reflected the greatest agitation and shouted, "He is going to hell."

The next morning, in the service, I scanned the audience in vain for the doctor's radiant countenance. He didn't appear but attended the afternoon meeting, seemingly more eager than ever. After the service, he approached.

"You may have noticed," he said, "that I was absent from the morning service."

I nodded and he continued. "I had my Bible and was going out the door of my house in Hankow, but it seemed as if some unseen force thrust me down upon the floor in a passion of prayer for Dr. Chow. I'd hardly been able to sleep at all the night before, thinking of his near approach to eternity without Christ. So I knelt and cried aloud to God, literally weeping a puddle of tears. The paroxysm of agony continued for about an hour. Then it departed and I rose from my knees with absolute peace of heart and mind. Looking at the clock, I saw that it was 11:30 and realized that I was too late for the morning service. So I came to this service.

"Now, Brother Graham, what I want to see you about is to exact a promise from you that as soon as you are able to return down the river, you will go to Shanghai and call on this friend whose life hangs in the balance and minister Christ to him before he goes hence."

I promised him that I'd do this at my earliest convenience and that if I were delayed, I would ask some other Christian in Shanghai to go and perform this ministry.

That night, at the conclusion of the meetings, I took a ship down the river to my home near Nanking and after a few days of Bible conference in my own town of Chinkiang, I boarded a train and went to Shanghai. A wonderful friend named Dr. Thornton Stearns worked there. When I arrived, I phoned Dr. Stearns and arranged for him to meet me at the hospital so we could see the mathematics professor.

Promptly at 9 o'clock the following morning, my friend and I entered the hospital and went to the office of the registrar to seek the room number of the ailing professor. As the registrar began thumbing through his records, another young clerk entered and courteously asked whom we sought. I told him Dr. Chow Chia-Su, and he replied with a solemn face and a shake of the head, "Dr. Chow Chia-Su has left this earth."

The clerk came across the record at the same time and nodded agreement, showing us the yellow record sheet. There was a signed statement by the attending physician that Dr. Chow had left this life, but the thing that attracted my attention was the date and time. It was on February 9 at 11:30 a.m. When I first heard that our mathematics professor had passed away, I wondered for just a moment why the Lord had brought me here after the death had already occurred. But as soon as I saw the date and time, I told Dr. Stearns, "I know now that though you and I have missed seeing him, one day we shall meet the mathematics professor in Glory."

My friend asked me how I arrived at that conclusion. I told him that the Lord never lay a burden of prayer such as was described to me by Dr. Cheng of Hankow without intending to answer such prayer. The fact that the passing of Dr. Chow exactly coincided with the time that Dr. Cheng had arisen from his knees, relieved of his burden, gave double assurance that the prayer was in the Holy Spirit.

I bade Dr. Stearns goodbye and boarded the train and returned to my home, content to let the divine principle illustrated in this connection wait for eternity for its vindication. In the council of God, I was not required to wait that long. Only a few days afterward, I was asked to speak at a mission high school for girls in my own city.

The text that morning was from the 90th Psalm: "So teach us to number our days that we may apply our hearts unto wisdom." I completed the message with the story of the Chinese educator in Wuchang whose heart had overflowed with the love of Christ and who had called upon God with tears to save his friend. At the end of the story, I told them I felt certain, due to the prayer of this friend, that we should all have the pleasure of seeing Dr. Chow Chia-Su in Glory one day. As the name of the math professor slipped from my mouth, I noticed that there were signs of recognition in the audience of girls. But I realized that may not be surprising since he was a very eminent scholar and well-known in Nanking and the whole Yangtze Valley.

After the prayer of dismissal, the Chinese principal of the high school asked me if I would wait for her a moment in her office. This I agreed to do, and when she entered the office, she sat down on the other side of the desk from me and said,

"Mr. Graham, that is a very interesting story that you told at the last of your message this morning. The most interesting part of it is that I know the other half of it. The gentleman to whom you referred, who has now passed away, is a son-in-law of this school. His wife is an alumna and incidentally a graduate of Columbia University of New York and a former principal. We call her Ai Loa [Love-Joy].

"Just a few days ago, she came into this very office to see me. I had not seen her for some time, and I had heard the report that her husband was dead. I found it difficult, therefore, to explain her peace and joy of countenance when she came in, coupled with the fact that she had on no widow's weeds or anything of that nature. I thought I must have been mistaken about her husband's death or she would not have appeared so calm and natural.

"After we had exchanged greetings, I said, 'And how is your husband? I heard that he was sick.'

"'Oh yes,' she replied, 'he is gone to be with Jesus, and I shall meet him in His presence one day.'

"I was very amazed at this statement," continued the principal, "because this couple were rather notoriously irreligious in our set, and how she could say so confidently that her husband had gone to be with Jesus and that she would meet him there, surprised me beyond words. So I asked her for the basis of her assurance.

"She replied, 'It is all very wonderful. I can't even explain it myself. My husband was at the point of death, and we all knew the end was near. He'd been comatose all of that Sunday morning. At about 10:30, as several of us stood around the room, he raised his head up off his pillow and with a very clear eye and voice declared to us all that he had seen Jesus Christ nailed on the cross for his sins. "I do not know why," he said, "the conviction has become so plain to me, but I know that I believe in Him. I know that I have eternal life and that I shall enter shortly into His presence. My dear wife," he said, addressing me, "we have wasted our lives. We have known of this Gospel but have neglected it. I urge you here and now, before I go hence, to trust Jesus Christ for salvation and to give your life to make Him known. In the school that we own and operate in Nanking, see to it that you have true Christian ministers come there and preach the Gospel to our students from now on."

"'After so charging us, he put his head back on the pillow, his lips began to move, and we could hear presently the tones of a gospel song he had learned long ago but which I had never heard him sing. We were confounded at the strength and clarity of his voice and when the song was over, he drew from somewhere in long hidden archives of his memory and quoted the entire chapter of 1 Corinthians 13. And as he clearly spoke these words, his spirit fled from his body and he was drawn into the presence of the Savior whom he had so recently trusted.'

"So, Mr. Graham," said the principal, "your judgment is correct. We shall see Dr. Chow one day in the Glory."

It is strange how astonished we can be about that which

we even claim to expect. My heart was filled with a song. I never reached the bedside of Dr. Chow in time, but the Holy Spirit, the Regenerator who leads humans to Christ, preceded me and did a much better job than I could have done. It happened that a few days later I met the lovely wife of the deceased mathematics professor and heard from her own lips the testimony of God's grace to her husband, to herself, and to her husband's brother, all because of the effectual, fervent prayer of a friend whose heart was broken with the love of Christ.

Written by one of Jimmy Graham's brothers
in the somewhat formal prose of the late 1800s,
the following is a description of the exemplary home
in which the Grahams grew up.

THE OLD MANSE

BY TUCKER GRAHAM

THE IDEAL HOME
"LEARN TO SHOW PIETY AT HOME"
1 TIMOTHY 5:4

Beyond the blue mountains, in the lovely valleys of the Shenandoah stands an old Manse about which cluster memories sacred and inspiring. It is deserted now, for the good pastor has finished his work among men, and the beloved companion of his life and labors for well-nigh fifty golden years was one of the white-robed company who waited to welcome his entry into that other home from which "they shall go no more out."

But this now silent Manse was long a vital center of spiritual and, in the best sense, also of social life in that community. Over its threshold passed not seldom men of rare gifts and of broadest culture and women admired for their charm of manner and their grace of character. Often in that family circle was eager youth privileged to hear the great problems that vexed Church or State discussed by men of master mind and acknowledged leadership. And when that quiet valley was swept by the fierce storm of war—the young cavalier and the grave commander of armies—men who were just winning their spurs and the man whose fame had belted the globe [Stonewall Jackson]—found welcome at the Manse, and in the intervals of march and battle passed many a delightful hour in company with the genial pastor and his gentle wife.

To the doors of the home through the long years came the weary and heavy-laden, the sin-sick and the heart sore, the discouraged and distressed from whatever cause. They came for counsel and went away with a new hope in the heart and a new light in the eye, for they had talked with one who walked with God. From its gates the poor and needy were never turned empty away, for the minister's slender purse, like Sarepta's ancient curse, could share with others without stint and still provide for its own.

To its quiet halls came young and old with the story of their blessings and their joys, for the pastor and his wife were as ready to rejoice with those that rejoiced as to weep with them that wept. Indeed, in the atmosphere of that home there was no trace of the gloom which some so strangely associate with the idea of religion— no measuring the strength of a man's faith by the length of his face. There was gladness as well as goodness there. Wit and wisdom were finely blended, and with a sense of the responsibilities of life was mingled the radiant joy of living. The genial humor of the father, the swift sally of wit and the rippling of laughter of the younger members of the household, lent brightness and color to the life of a home in which duty was the watchword, rigid integrity the rule of conduct, and faith in God the motivating power.

Moreover, it was a busy home as well as a bright and happy one. No drone was permitted in that domestic hive. Son and daughter each had an appropriate task, and was expected to contribute cheerfully a fair quota of service. Thus slender resources were largely neutralized by a wise division of labor, and each was taught to bear a definite share in the making of the home. And now, from their own widely separated homes, they look back to the happy days of youth and rejoice in the necessity that compelled and the kindly wisdom that directed this useful training.

Nor was the spiritual nature forgotten in that valley home. The recent folly that fails to require attendance at church lest "the children acquire a distaste for religion," found no echo in that home. Absence from church or Sabbath school was as rare as absence from dinner. Church attendance was an essential part of the life of young and old alike.

On Sabbath afternoons the children, forbidden to roam the streets, gathered about the mother for personal instruction. Passages of Scripture, the Catechism, and the grand old hymns of the church were memorized and recited. Much of the time was spent in reading selected books or other interesting matter. But novels and secular publications of every kind were banished on the Lord's Day. It may not be inappropriate to add that there were always fruits or sweets for the children on Sunday afternoon, and a time for pleasant chat. The purpose, successful to a very marked degree, was to make Sunday distinct from all other days in its atmosphere and occupation, and at the same time a day cheerful and attractive—not somber and repelling.

The minister was a diligent and systematic student. He believed that a sermon that had not wearied the preacher in its preparation was sure to weary the people in its delivery. His sermons were the product of a cultured mind, forceful and scholarly, highly spiritual and helpful. They were delivered with grace and impressiveness in a voice clear, musical, and winning, and in language chaste and beautiful to a rare degree. So well-rounded were his discourses that they were as ready for the printer as for the pulpit when he laid down his pen. Yet he modestly shrank from the use of printer's ink and seldom yielded to the request of friends to be allowed to publish some particularly striking discourse.

As a pastor he was profoundly beloved. His very presence was a benediction. Old and young rejoiced at his coming and found cheer and comfort in the kindly ministry of one who, like his Master, went about doing good. And he was every inch a man. Gentle yet firm, kindly yet courageous, there was about him that quality of manhood which men everywhere recognize without effort and reverence without stint. With a face so handsome that it would attract attention in a crowd, a graceful carriage, a rare tact, a manner so gracious and frank and kindly that all were irresistibly drawn to him, he was far more than three score years the leading citizen of his city and section. Men and women of that older day looked upon him as the ideal man. Their children and their children's children came under his influence, felt the charm of his personality and in after years blessed God for the lasting impression of his character upon their hearts. People of the world, often critical and censorious of others, were hushed to silence in his presence "and as they looked upon him, took knowledge of him that he had been with Jesus."

This is but a meager pen-portrait of the master of the home as we were privileged to know him in the golden years now gone. None who knew and loved him, whether in the vigorous days of early manhood, or in the mellow eventide when the years had silvered his head, will think the picture overdrawn.

But it takes two to make a home, whether manse or mansion, cottage or palace. This minister was peculiarly blessed in the gentlewoman who won his heart and graced his home. She was a helpmate indeed. None knew her but to love her; none named her but to praise. She shared in all the work of her husband's church. She went with him on his pastoral rounds and in his absence went alone to visit the sick and sorrowing, or to welcome the stranger. Wherever the shadows of grief or trial fell thickest, there she came with the radiance of her gracious spirit to cheer and to help, and through the long years a great company of the rich and the poor, the cultured and the uncultured, have been quick to rise up and call her blessed.

Here was an extremely busy life. The crowded hours flew past, each with its special duty. The salary was meager—the children many. The sewing for this large family was almost altogether done by the mother. The housework was directed by her, and at times done with her own hands. She was a notable housekeeper, and her home was a center of generous hospitality, even in a community famed for its hospitable homes.

To accomplish so many things and to do them all so well, while maintaining her charm of spirit, her genial flow of humor, and her unobtrusive interest in all that concerned her neighbors and friends, is a rare achievement. What then was the secret of a life of such singular sweetness and power? The answer is not far to seek. The "beauty of holiness" was reflected in her life because she lingered long in the audience chamber of the great King. Kneeling at His footstool, she communed with Him whom her soul loved, and learned thus to serve or suffer with serene and quiet courage.

Because her days were crowded it was her habit to rise in the early hours of the morning, before the members of the household were astir, and at a rocking chair in the corner of the bedchamber kneel and pour out her soul in prayer to the Father in heaven. If one of the children chanced to rise earlier than usual and to pass through that chamber, his eyes turned instinctively toward a kneeling mother's figure in that quiet corner. Often he caught upon the mother's face the glint of a light that was "never on sea or land." Or perchance tears were upon the cheek and he heard his own name spoken in prayer as she pled with God for her boy.

Thus, the key to her singularly rich and fruitful nature was that her life was hid with Christ in God. The fires of faith and love that burned so brightly in her heart were kindled at the altar of the Eternal. Prayer was the golden clasp that bound together the volume of her life. The morning set the keynote of the day, and out of her Holy of Holies she came to take up anew the tangled web of life—

serene and strong, unfevered, unfretted, and unafraid.

One other there was in that home who was gladly reckoned a member of that family circle and added much richness and beauty to its life. This was the mother's mother. From the midst of a group of those who served their generation well, a face of wondrous charm looks down upon me from my study wall as I write. Whether the world would call it beautiful, I don't know. Yet no one who ever looked upon that face in life or even as its features have been preserved by photographs, could fail to look again. A friend once described it with unique aptness as "a love letter to the whole world." It was indeed the mirror of a soul in which the Scripture graces were blended in a personality of rare beauty and charm.

The inheritor of intellect and culture, of wealth and social position, she entered with unreserved delight into those forms of social pleasure of which her Christian judgment approved. Without seeking it, and perhaps without even realizing it, she was ever accorded the central place in any gathering in which she might be found.

But she took joy most of all in the service of her Redeemer. The sanctuary was her delight and she was an active participant in all its work. More than sixty years have come and gone since she gathered the children of the Manse about her and told them the story of the Christ child, and of those other heroes of Bible days, with such marvelous skill that the picture of that eager face abides and the sound of her gentle voice still rings through our memories.

At length the day came when her allotted task was done and, while the bells were calling folks to the House of God, she heard the call to higher service, and passed from the home on earth to the mansions eternal. Is it any wonder that some who, as guests, tarried there for a season long ago recall the event as one of the unique and uplifting experiences of a lifetime? Is it strange that those who were privileged to call it home dwell with tender gratitude upon the priceless memories that cluster there? Five sons and two daughters were born and reared in that home. When the sons reached maturity and passed over its threshold to do a man's work in the world, they bore with them the benediction of a noble father's face and were encompassed with a mother's prayers. Is it a surprising thing that three of these sons became ministers of the Great Evangel and the others have been called to bear office in the church of God?

Are homes like this a vanishing asset in our church and national life today? The Christian home is the cornerstone upon which the church and the republic alike are built. To suffer it to perish is to invite disaster. It was the sweet singer of the Scottish hills who looked in upon a household that placed God at the heart of its family life, and then wrote this tribute to the Christian home:

> "FROM SCENES LIKE THESE
> OLD SCOTIA'S GRANDEUR SPRINGS,
> THAT MAKES HER LOVED AT HOME,
> REVERED ABROAD;
> PRINCES AND LORDS ARE BUT THE BREATH
> OF KINGS,
> AN HONEST MAN'S
> THE NOBLEST WORK OF GOD."

STEPHEN FORTOSIS is the author of *Great Men and Women of the Bible, A Treasury of Great Christian Stories,* and several other books. He has taught at Western Seminary and Trinity International University and holds an M.A. and a Ph.D. in religious education from Talbot School of Theology in California. He currently resides in Florida with his wife and two children.

MARY GRAHAM REID and her husband served for 36 years as missionaries to Japan. The granddaughter of Jimmy Graham II and the daughter of James Graham III, she spent much of her childhood in China. John and Mary Reid live in a retirement community in Little Rock, Arkansas.

ROBERTSON MCQUILKIN (Afterword) was president of Columbia International University for 22 years. Formerly a missionary to Japan, he is author of *The Great Omission, Life in the Spirit, A Promise Kept,* and other books. He lives with his wife in Columbia, South Carolina.